Rivers & Birds

Recent Books by Merrill Gilfillan

River Through Rivertown (Poems)
Magpie Rising: Sketches from the Great Plains
Sworn Before Cranes
Burnt House to Paw Paw: Appalachian Notes
Satin Street (Poems)
Chokecherry Places: Essays from the High Plains
Grasshopper Falls
The Seasons (Poems)
Small Weathers (Poems)

Rivers & Birds

Merrill Gilfillan

Merrill Gilfillan (signature)

Johnson Books

BOULDER

An earlier version of "The Mississippi to Hannibal" appeared in the *Wapsipinicon
Almanac*. Thanks to Tim Fay, the editor.

Published by Johnson Books, a division of Johnson Publishing Company,
1880 South 57th Court, Boulder, Colorado 80301. Visit our website at
www.JohnsonBooks.com. E-mail: books@jpcolorado.com.

9   8   7   6   5   4   3   2   1

Cover painting: *Black-crowned Night-Heron* by Stuart Gentling and Scott
Gentling. From *Of Birds and Texas*, University of Texas Press, 2001.
Author photo by Ken Abbott.

Library of Congress Cataloging-in-Publication Data
Gilfillan, Merrill, 1945–
    Rivers and birds / Merrill Gilfillan.
        p. cm.
    ISBN 1-55566-296-X
  1. Natural History—United States. 2. Bird watching—United States.
3. Gilfillan, Merrill, 1945—Journeys—United States. I. Title.
    QH104.G55 2003
    508.73—dc21   2003011138

Printed in the United States by
Johnson Printing
1880 South 57th Court
Boulder, Colorado 80301

Printed on ECF paper with soy ink

Contents

The Musselshell & South   1

Sparrows in Winter   11

Rain on the Catskills   19

A Visit to Four or Five Streams   27

Swamp Angels   37

The Mississippi to Hannibal   45

Blackcaps in the Fall   67

Prairie Proper   75

A Clear Day on Plum Island   83

Timpas Creek   87

Going Back in May   97

A Black Hills Loop   107

Short Days: Birds & the Turn of the Year   115

From Summer Notebooks: Sun Dance Notes   125

Works Consulted   137

The Musselshell & South

for Ken McCullough

You will almost always see a hobo or two or three as you
drive the "Highline" of route 2 across northern Montana.
I noticed a pair yesterday just outside Cut Bank, resting
under a cottonwood. Montana has historically been a place
of many footloose men. I think it results from a combination of the great and varied space of its latitudes with that
peculiar, teasing phenomenon of border-drawn-in-the-dirt.
Cut Bank in the old train-wealthy days of the early twentieth
century was known as a hobo axis, with thriving camps at
various edges of town. It seems it was logistically sited as a
spot to rest up for, or from, a boxcar crossing of the Rockies
just to the west. As well as being thirty or forty miles from
the Canadian border, an important psychological factor for
the skeptical marginal citizen. There is a current academic
discipline known as "border studies." I believe it concerns
itself thus far mostly with the U.S.-Mexican line, but it is a
safe bet that this northern demarcation sees some very
interesting and little-known osmosis, as it has since the
days of the Louis Riel rebellion and the back-and-forth of

some of those Métis peoples, and certain enterprising Blackfoot families who managed to sign up for residence and reimbursement on both sides of the playful border. In any event, along with Sidney, Nebraska, down on the Union Pacific Line, where I often see a group of mobile men and inexpensive pup tents camped in the Russian olives west of town along the tracks, the Montana highline is still a hobo habitat, in case anyone wants to load the kiddies into the car and drive them out to witness men who care not a whit for indoor plumbing and carry not the Television Look on their faces …

It is the first real cold snap of the fall. A Canadian front dropping south. And no doubt many of the hoboes dropping south along with it. It is some three weeks after the World Trade Center attacks, and I have been taking a drive. As I started south myself I opted to do so via the Musselshell River route, to pace things and to partake of its company. This morning I cut across through Lewistown to the hamlet of Mosby and drove south on the patchy variable-medium road that ascends that river, a lovely and lonely road rolling high above the valley, a road you will remember with childish affection, hill and dale following the beacons of the October cottonwoods some forty miles, and then into another hamlet with the Hardyesque name of Melstone, at which point in younger times I might well have turned around and driven it back downstream just for the oxygenating kinetics.

But today I turn west and continue along the river, after its big swinging bend, on highway 12. As always, the Musselshell strikes one as a modest river with not a trace of swagger. The valley, likewise, is pleasant without histrionics, a mix of amenable cottonwood groves and pine-covered bluffs on the south side. Haystacks at the ready, a little tillage. Herds of horses, red cattle and black cattle, sheep.

I eventually find a public fishing access along the river, a place they call Asparagus Point, and drive back in there. An aggressive band of beavers has been busy along the stream, has dropped half a dozen cottonwoods two feet through and is working on four or five more. One of them smells so fresh it could have fallen last midnight. I stroll downstream along several sharp bends, past a fifteen-by-fifteen-foot cabin ruin, to a quiet place across from sizable shale cliffs where a steady sloughing of stone goes on, it seems, with great regularity, and sit down by the Musselshell, sit in her company, amid the old cow plops.

And there is a little peace there, after the recent weeks of virulent "history" and its galactic, battery-acid images.

A monastic little peace in the quiet grove and the robin flocks along the river, pushed down by the cold front and now bathing in the shallows by the score. And the neighborhood god is a pleasantly preoccupied leprechaun/kingfisher hybrid just downstream who, although tough on the minnows, wouldn't hurt a flea.

Overhead, some of the thinnest, most evenly laced cosmic doilies of cirrus.

I slept in the town of Roundup and after breakfast and an anachronistic piece of warm sweet-potato pie went on in the morning at first light, on upstream. More chunks of stone recently fallen toward the river. A dead porcupine. Cattails of many colors. Up through pines and out onto high plains-meadow, and suddenly the Big Snowy range far to the right. I drove down the Dean Creek road to look at the Musselshell a minute. There were a dozen mule deer feeding in the north-side meadow, and a dozen whitetails on the south. A coyote howling, and more of those soft, round, piney bluffs along the edge of the stream. They could have called it the "Pretty Shoulders River."

Over toward Lavinia the Crazy Mountains showed up straight ahead, elegant, self-possessed, and then the Beartooth range in the distant southwest. Lavinia has a handsome old hotel, the Adams, still surprisingly spruce and white, though the rail tracks in front have long been pulled up, and the old well-read grouse hunters who probably de-trained there have long been muttering by other fires. Just south of town I stopped for a last look at the river. Large congregations of Canada geese were feeding in the bottoms, and then off in a discrete corner I saw four sandhill cranes—big birds, full man-sized, they must have been of the greater sandhill subspecies. They saw me at the bridge, of course, and stiffened indignantly as they watched.

Farther south, there appeared suddenly out of the ranch hills a most violent man in a dented pickup who swerved around me as I sat parked on the shoulder of the road mak-ing notes. His face was ugly and wild, and his curse was vicious, stunning, even through a closed window.

And on toward Billings. I remembered those four cranes, the size of them, all watching me as I stood by the bridge, their hackles up, moving slowly away in carefully coordinated giant steps. And the truck at the motel in Roundup with a rear license plate holder that read "Catkiller" on the top and "Vietnam Class of 67" on the bottom. I decided to drive straight on down to the Plenty Coups house on the Crow reservation and eat lunch there.

Plenty Coups was the last of the old-time Crow chiefs. He had this nice square-log house built for himself and his family in the late 1880s, adding to it over the next quarter century. A two-story structure with a pair of dormer windows above the front porch, which faces east and has a grand view of the Pryor Mountains to the south. It is now a state-maintained historical area at the outskirts of Pryor village, Pryor of the leaning off-season tepee poles and thousand burrito wrappers and pretty red roans.

I stop for a few minutes by the high school as I drive in. There is a Saturday-afternoon football game in progress. Eight-man. The Plenty Coups Warriors versus a team from up north, way up near Lewistown. It is a perfectly temperatured day, golden trees and cloudless sky. Someone made a joke about the Crow team's delay-of-game penalty and the "Indian time" factor.

I can hear an occasional huzzah from the field now and then even as I eat my sandwich at a picnic table over on the grounds of the chief's house. Desiccated box elder leaves rustle overhead in the still afternoon. The house, now a museum, is closed for the season, but I remember from the one time I visited it that Plenty Coups's spirit animal was not an eagle or a grizzly or a bull elk but a chickadee. It seems to mark the distinctive intelligence and nature of the man.

The house today makes me think of the rather similar house built for Quanah Parker down near Cache, Oklahoma. A similar look, as I recall, under similar hail-to-the-chief circumstances, from about the same period. And brings to mind the great Quanah story. The agent for the Comanches strongly hoped that their leader would set a good example for the tribe's transition to reservation life and European mores. Quanah at the time had several wives. The agent strenuously advised him to change that state of affairs: "You've got to tell all but one wife to leave." Quanah, after a moment's consideration: "*You* tell them."

The Bighorns gradually and surely take over the southern vista as you drop down from the north. Yesterday they shone with recent snow, bulged across a third of the horizon like a cetacean polar cap. I remember the mild shock I received when I first realized that Custer's men on their last hill had such a full-force view of them. From the St. Xavier road they loom like Subasio over Assisi, with the cold, sky-locked, upward stare that brought them, somewhere along the line, the Medicine Wheel, that rough-hewn cog-gear in some great intuited clockwork.

I spent the night in Sheridan and got an early start this morning. There was one more gestural stop I wanted to make, a pause before resigning myself to the interstate and the long day home. I took old highway 87 south from town, down through Banner and Story and out the pretty road to the site of the Wagon Box fight. It is another sunny morning, a Sunday, and the early goblins and corpses of Halloween are to be seen hanging from trees or sprawled on yards and porches.

The Wagon Box fight took place in August 1867 on this high plateau between Big and Little Piney Creeks, a few miles from Fort Phil Kearney, when Lakotas under Crazy Horse and Hump attacked and engaged a group of wood cutters and their protecting soldiers, who took shelter in the rudimentary "fort" of army-wagon boxes set in a small oval. A half day of charges, a few casualties on each side, and a herd of army mules for the Indians. A chorus of Lakota women watched the action from a pointy hill to the east. A place with five hours of History, *accompli*, for now; done for and long cooled. There is a remarkably spacious view to the north and east from the battle site. To the west, the steep foothills, the variegated brightness I associate with these eastern Bighorns: varied textures and tones and humidities ranging from the succulent aspen drainages to dark pine slopes to bone-dry hills and snowfields. Three horses graze beyond the fence, and a few magpies waddle

about. It is well lit and breezy, more like a March day. The
meadowlarks sing heartily in hurry-up, catch-up time.

One of the signs describing the battle discusses the pos-
sibility that this is not the exact site of the encounter; there
has been from the beginning, it seems, debate over the pre-
cise location on the plateau of the wagon-box corral, even
when the participants themselves returned to mark it. We
are standing on speculative soil. Even my paltry memory of
a visit here some ten years ago is utterly different from the
place I see this morning; I recalled it vaguely as a rather
modest opening surrounded by mixed aspen groves. That
might well be the residue of a fanciful illustration in a boy-
hood book on the Indian wars.

The confusion is bracing, and after I walk the brief visitors' loop a half-dozen times, the events of 1867 begin to
fade noticeably. I find myself thinking about a down-to-
earth good meal.

The white-crowned sparrows along Piney Creek are
restless. The hoboes to the north are stirring, turning up
the collars of their coats. Those cranes near the Musselshell. And myself. All of us getting ready, turning antidot-
ally south.

Sparrows in Winter

A lovely young woman once wrote, "The canyon in winter is the color of a sparrow." I often think of that connection in the cold season—both terminals of the metaphor. Much of the December landscape, even in the flatlands, fits the deceptively simple description; at the same time, the wintering sparrow flocks provide a welcome injection of both activity—fundamental stirring—and companionate hue.

This morning, in the week after Christmas, still shows spotty remnants of snow, but the sun is bright, and it raises the faded colors of the countryside to a modest but primary richness. The endless variations of straw-beiges in the grasses and bony weeds. The summer crimson of osiers now a drained apple-red, and the willows a vague apricot wash against the cottonwoods' close-to-the-chest midwinter gray. To the west, the snowy Front Range of the Rockies is almost too bright to look at. The starlings are brilliant in the full light, have never looked better. Last summer's flattened sage and crusty mullein stalks have rarely looked worse.

Most all the ponds in this former gravel quarry are frozen solid and snow-covered. Around and across one of them a coyote's track wanders, edging the cattails: a sniff here, a brief consideration and a slight digression there, then off, beeline, across the ice to the far side, beckoned by some invisible promising latency. And on to the southeast, following the nose in a fearless celebration of the mock-random, open to anything the morning might have to offer.

Coyotes are such a familiar part of my days, sometimes remarked with such nonchalance, it is as if I have known them forever rather than just two decades. They are nearly a daily feature. I think of certain individual coyotes now and again as I would a memorable face glimpsed long ago on a city street. There is a group of three I encounter every month or so. They inhabit open grassland country and hang around an old house foundation—scattered chunks of masonry and remnant riverstone walls, even a pair of left-behind Russian olive trees. One is a dark old fellow of belligerent mien; I can sense the low territorial growl in his throat from a hundred yards. There is a pale female, and a carefree younger one that pays me little mind. And that is their house and home; any child could see they'd taken over the premises, moved right in.

Then there is the solitary pup I surprised one morning as I topped a far-flung eastern Colorado rise. It sat there on its haunches looking both sleepy and lonesome, seemed even happy to see me. I stopped to watch, and it began walking toward me, blinking its sleepy eyes as a cat might when crossing a room in hopes of an ear scratch. It came within fifteen yards before the instinct grapple caught and it paused to study me more skeptically, finally drifted off, stopping and starting, then ambled away over the hill.

And a ravaged one I saw in the middle of highway 50 down in the Arkansas valley that had just been struck by car or truck and was making a valiant effort to raise itself from the pavement, its hindquarters crushed, looking wildly up at the sky as heavy traffic roared by with a look on its face for which there was only one caption: "What the Fuck and What the Fucking World?"

So when a flock of tree sparrows jumps from the ground to a wild plum bush it is time to take them in for a minute or two through the glasses, take note, as a kind of December relish. The bright, almost rufous chestnut; the subtle smudge of rusty-buff on the sides; the broken "partial" wingbars against the rich browns that annually bring to mind the pattern of the checkerspot butterfly.

After my first May in the West I turned instinctively to the sparrow tribe, out of a sort of desperation, when I realized how stark was the absence of warbler passage along the Front Range of Colorado. I needed a replacement in a hurry, a replacement of depth and intricacy, and the sparrows have served well in all dimensions ever since.

In those days the lark sparrow, near at hand, was quite new to me and offered itself as the most striking, even warbler-like in brash configuration, of sparrows. To catch the subtleties of the Brewer's and clay-colored became a regular spring migration feature. The fine points, the easily overlooked flecks and daubs of color, emerged as keystones to be watched for; to mark the dull chestnut spot on the vesper's shoulder and the little yellow pip on the grasshopper sparrow's wing was now the equivalent of catching the crimson smudge on a Nashville warbler's crown.

Soon there were excursions to locate some of the more specialized species. To western Wyoming for the sage sparrow; a long safari to the northern plains for Baird's and Leconte's. The first Cassin's outside Muleshoe, Texas. And of course Arizona for its xeric specialties: the black-chinned, the rufous-crowned, and the rufous-winged.

But now that I pause to consider and shuffle through the array, the most demanding of the thirty-five-odd North American sparrows, the one whose searching out I think of with actual surprise—surprise at the sudden blitzkrieg intensity of the project—is the five-striped.

That was an expedition good to remember on a winter's day. I had been wandering about southeastern Arizona for a week, moving from one legendary birding spot to another. The Chiricahuas, Madera Canyon, Sonoita Creek. Waiting at the city dump in Sells for the caracaras to come in. As always in that edge of the country, it was a case of continual awe, such a new world that border country holds. Becards and trogons and tyrannulets. All day the endless looking, and on into the night. It is a saturation, and on this particular May morning I had ducked into Patagonia's Museum of the Horse for both the air conditioning and a freshening change of scale.

I was trying to decide if I had had enough. Finally, debating on the sidewalk in Patagonia, I opted, as long as I was in the neighborhood, to take another day, go down and have a look at Sycamore Canyon; a look for, among other things, the five-striped sparrow, a species found in just a few carefully selected habitats in Arizona, rarely more than a few miles north of the Mexican boundary. I loaded up on water and knapsack food and drove down, over west of Ruby, to the canyon trailhead. I was looking at the map posted there when another birder showed up, a young man from southern California. We talked, compared notes on what we had heard of the descent, and decided to go down together, camp when night came on, and continue to the bottom early next morning.

It was midafternoon. We carried minimal packs and sleeping bags and as much water as we could manage. It was rough going in many places: boulder-hopping along the mostly dry streambed, hard on the legs and relentless on the attention. Sycamore is notorious for several varieties of rattlesnake; we had both heard that. There were steep eight-foot drops and one or two unskirtable pools of sweet, waist-deep water to be waded. It was a lovely, trogon-accompanied descent, down and down, with the distinct sensation of getting a little wilder at every step. My partner was a thorough birder. He recorded each avian occurrence into a small tape recorder, sotto voce, in a sort of golf announcer's voice that lent the entire enterprise a pleasantly absurd "observed" perspective.

Late afternoon we chose a roomy, rock-free sandbar in the streambed and spread out our bags. We ate a meal of peanut butter and lemons, or some such, and then fell asleep to the soft hoots and chuckles of some of the most exotic owls in America.

At daybreak we hurried on down and in an hour reached the flimsy barbed-wire fence marking the border of Sonora. And just above the boundary, on a booming Sycamore canyon side, the five-striped started to sing, and we tracked it down, located it sitting on an ocotillo tip, the famous stripes flowing back from the bill. ...

Such a spontaneous, clean, mission-accomplished outing through such noble terrain. After resting a half hour I said good-bye to my friend—he sat in a squiggle of shade updating his recorder—climbed straight back up the canyon, reaching the cars about noon, and drove away toward Tucson.

Sparrows in December or February stand for all that: latency and memory-footings. That is one of the reasons these ten white-crowned sparrows lurking in the chill currant bush bear such wealthy tidings. They stand for emblazonry in the fallow season.

As I watch them for a moment I recall a small, boxed, battery-operated game of bird recognition I had as a child: two wires to touch to metal terminals, match the names with the pictures on cardboard sheets, a red bulb lights upon success. But it's the lightly schematized, painterly rich representations of the birds that come to mind, their stylized stripes and scalings stretching over fifty years, their promise of an engaging world available just beyond the frosty windows.

When I get home I will make coffee and pull down an old bird book or two, something from the past century; maybe browse through the Brooks and Fuertes plates in *The Birds of Massachusetts*, sparrows and beyond.

Rain on the Catskills

It was raining in Port Jervis, down on the Delaware, and in Cahoonzie, and in Forestburg, New York. Light, needling rain for the most part, but the weatherman at noon predicted it would be around for the next three days—the three October days I had set aside for the Catskills. I drove through Monticello slowly, and then again. It had an appealing soggy-leaf-on-the-sidewalk look. There was a big old hotel and a pair of veteran diners on the main street. The town was a short drive south of the central Catskills. I decided to hole up in Monticello and see what happened.

I took a room in a newer wing of the hotel that smelled unabashedly of Pall Mall smoke and cloaca maxima. The combination slapped you at the door. But then Catskill birding, New England birding, means birding in the grand tradition: well-loved, well-observed, well-annotated country, pedigreed in every respect. I knew I would rather engage it through malodorous drizzle than not at all.

After a nap I shook out the poncho, bought local apples, and drove slowly north toward Fallsburg to see the Neversink River, a good rainy-day destination. There is a public access point not far from the village, and I walked a stretch of the stream through heavy mist. She is a mossy, unruffled river, pretty and preoccupied, carrying thousands of pale maple leaves. On the slope above, alders and birch drooped and dripped.

Out along the road one of those striking old men with Walt Whitman beards and flop hats strode along with a bulging bag of crushed cans over his shoulder. Those fellows would become almost a signature of the Catskills, due to their unapologetic numbers and their forthright bearing.

The outer Catskills region is a cultural mosaic of almost insolent mix. Driving aimlessly back toward Monticello, I passed through a water-logged, pop-up landscape of scruffy, mildewed old Hebrew summer camps huddled within lacer-atingly suggestive chain-link fences; wobbly ranks of "bungalow colonies," soot-streaked and hollow-eyed; detox facilities beside a well-heeled yoga grounds; low-eaved taverns and apple stands; rambling resort hotels no longer young; and hard-pressed rural dwellings. Exotic-dancer joints. Bingo parlors. Judaica shops. It all appears unable to explain how it ended up here in the Neversink drainage.

Back in the hotel I studied the maps, then walked over to the nearest diner, where I bought the final serving of baked ziti from a large battered pan.

The next morning I drove into the mountains—light drizzle—and up the East Fork of the Neversink to hike a little. Six or seven miles above the fork, I started walking up an old logging road stony and wet enough to pass for a bona fide riverbed. Hemlock and beech on both sides. What birds there were fed glumly in the understory— kinglets and white-throats. Blue jays called consolingly in the damp distances. The adverb is apt; I had just driven up from the South, and jays were vocalizing all the way. It is not just the steady accompaniment of practical song, not simply a year-round, rain-or-shine presence. It stands as a conversation of high vocabulary and enormous range, even intellectual content, from wheedle to lullaby, mutter to scuttlebutt, query to jeer.

I tend to forget the rawness of much of rural New England—as wild as any part of the poorer Appalachians: tough, patchwork steads with huge piles of firewood against their walls, a threadbare nibble-agriculture featuring a blend of thin sheep and woolly chickens.

I walked for an hour. No one else was about. Eventually I struck the East Fork again, stood on a little bridge in a valley opening, and watched her regular accipiter-like oscillation of flutter and glide. I had hoped the weather would force some late warblers down, stall a flock right there in the Catskills, but except for a single myrtle warbler on the south side of the stream, there were none.

Low clouds and easy rain can induce intense warblering. I remember misty spring mornings in the Midwest—or perhaps it was a single beneficent morning that has reproduced kaleidoscopically over a decade, so intense it was— when the forest was loud with song: chestnut-sideds, redstarts, hoodeds. I gradually realized I was in the midst of a great flock. And just then the rain increased to a steady light shower, enough that I took shelter beneath a young beech tree, and that brought the birds down, the entire flock feeding ten or fifteen feet above the ground and close at hand—black-throated blues and greens, magnolias, Canadas. So many birds it was impossible to keep up with them. Binoculars were hardly needed.

But not that day in the Catskills. I drove down to Claryville and bought a coffee to go, stopped at the old tannery ruins outside town, where hemlock bark was used in preparing saddles and other gear for the Grand Army of the Republic, then drove over the hump to the Willowemoc Road. The recent rain had stripped most Catskills trees of half their leaves, and when I rounded a bend and encountered one of the more intact slopes, heavy with yellow popple, it was as if the sun had suddenly burst through.

At a cindery pull-off overlooking Willowemoc Creek, it was raining hard enough that I was forced to bird from the car—lower the passenger-side window halfway and from low in the seat watch the treetops along the stream. This is a low-grade form of the pastime, roughly comparable to running in place. But these are the Catskills, and the call to see birds on estimable ornithological ground can build to urgency. When I stopped decades ago at the Oakley Plantation in Louisiana, where Audubon spent a season collecting and painting birds, after touring the outbuildings—the "pigeonière" and the "garconière" and the cookhouse—and walking quietly through the fine home and leaning respectfully into the small room where John James had abided, thinking of both the extent and the amicable finitude of his great project—"I will paint the Birds of America, A to Z, and be done with it"—the need to find and focus on a bird of merit was inordinately strong, and I struck off into the sleepy woods on the Oakley grounds and worked them through and through until a yellow-throated vireo began to chorus high in one of the slender trees. …

After twenty minutes I rolled up the window and left Willowemoc and drove down and west, over to the Beaverkill to find a similar place beside it, a place below Roscoe with cheery orange sumac on one side and a view of the river on the other. There were fishermen out in mid-stream. On the far slopes an occasional tree held lacy yellow foliage that looked like scattered bursts of gentle fireworks against the dark hills. Chickadees and crows. I counted my cash and started a crossword from the *Times*.

It was the same the next day. A walk in the poncho somewhere in the Peekamoose neighborhood, then a drive up to Big Indian, barberries glowing brightly in the low light of the stream bottoms. The Catskills reservoirs are brimful, water for Manhattan and the boroughs. In Big Indian, another coffee in the car in the little town park. The mountains all morning had been handsome enough with their upper reaches lost in the clouds. I recalled a spring day some years ago when I took friends visiting from California into the Black Hills, with a stop at Mt. Rushmore, only to find the giant heads hidden in dense fog from about the sternums up, and we quoted Basho—

> In a way
> it was even better
> not seeing Mt. Fuji
> in foggy rain.

Restless and tired of birding from the car, I drove out from the mountains and up to Roxbury to visit John Burroughs's Woodchuck Lodge and grave site, all sopping wet, where I thought of my favorite essay of his, "A Hunt for the Nightingale," in which more than anyplace else the plasticity of the writing matches the goodness of the heart and the sharpness of the eye, and on up route 30 a ways, looking for something to do. When the rain lightened, I walked a half mile along the highway and the East Fork of the Delaware River. There was a flash of waxwings overhead, and then, from a small, tight alder swamp, four ducks flushed, and they were black ducks, and they saved the soggy day. I hadn't seen a black duck in probably twenty years; but I remember it perfectly, so black duck it was, hiding cannily in a similar woody pothole, watching me pass, watching my eyes, watching the odds and angles, slyly maneuvering to hide itself. Black ducks: the chariest, most reclusive of their kind. "Sagacious" they have been called by people who knew. Numbers declining, but ... *Violet speculum.* Hardly a warbler; a classic New England occasion all the same.

The ducks and their leap from the alders broke the seal of expectancy, released some vague pressure. I mobilized to move on, head over to the Berkshires and friends. I drove back through the mountains, easterly, and stopped one last time not far from Tannersville, pulled off along the road for a sandwich and a final have-at-it. It was a pleasure just to turn off the windshield wipers for a while. Last chance for Catskills warblers. But I found myself wondering more if the hotel effluvium that had osmosed into all my clothing would ever wash away. I was getting a little cranky and downright lonesome. Then a sooty, double-jointed semi truck slowed, sidled hedgingly into the pull-off beside me, looking for a snooze or a phone call. Company!

I wiped the window with my sleeve to make out the big peeling letters on the smudgy, swaybacked bed. Ah! a load of solid waste from the metro seaboard, with one "D. Murgo" at the helm.

A Visit to Four or Five Streams

for Jim Harrison

I happened across an odd book some months ago while browsing in the nonfiction part of the public library. The title—*Pale Ink*—caught my eye. Authored by Henriette Mertz and published in 1953, it is an airy, sleuthful account of ancient Chinese explorations, several of which, according to Mertz's reading of the legendary old texts, set extended foot on the American West, including the New Mexican mountains.

I thought of it this morning as I drove west from Mills, New Mexico, on a gravel road with a good wide-angle view of much of the Sangre de Cristo range and other peaks, most with a fresh snow topping for the year, though today they shimmer in a late-November warm spell that has gone on in the region for what seems like many weeks.

This eastern New Mexico, the rolling plains, has patiently emerged as one of the patently unimpeded spaces in my experience. It carries an active apartness that approaches purity. The lay is always of interest, intrigue even, in its subtle shiftings and tonal variation. And the human population is extremely thin. It is a landscape of many widely spaced weed-run hulks and stony ruins.

I wanted to visit the Canadian River where it flows through the Kiowa National Grasslands in a deep place called Mills Canyon. The edge of the drop is some eight miles south and west from the onetime town of Mills, the edge where the grasslands give gradual way to scattered junipers and surfacing bedrock. At that point, signs warn of the volatile road to the bottom, so I parked and set off from there. The road soon drops into a many-canyoned, heavily conifered descent and for most of the way follows a prominent side canyon through rock-strewn slopes and down into chaparral hills spiked with the occasional belligerent cholla. It was half chilly in the shade, toasty on the sunny stretches. The pale scrub oak leaves lent just a hint of "fall color." I heard a flock of red crossbills pass overhead.

In forty minutes I was out on a point with an overlook view of the big valley and the river below, curving nimbly around a formidable stack of red and salmon stone. The slopes of the canyon are juniper- and piñon-dotted and swoop up nine hundred feet, they say, to a varied rim of reddish rock. And the Canadian itself, what I came along for, is of course an unmistakable plains river set by cold-blooded circumstance at the bottom of a rugged canyon.

Most of her cottonwoods were bare, but one or two over where she first came into sight still bore burnt-gold leaves. Any real chromatics were supplied by the willow stands and the salt cedars along her course.

Down near the river I found a place to sit. It had been warm enough steadily enough this season that a good many small insects and butterflies were still bumbling on the aimless wing. The woman in the Mills post office, where I had stopped to ask directions, was saying that the weather was so warm the bears couldn't get to sleep for hibernation, were wandering around in generally foul moods. The noon had the feel of a slightly out-of-place, Rip van Winkle autumn lull. Even the tree-toad trill from up the canyon wall had a somnolent sound to it.

I was sitting near a juniper bush laden with "cedar berries." They remind me of Walt Whitman, who considered titling one of his collections after those humble fruits. An odd place to think of Walt Whitman, but again, only slightly. The Canadian was at a low-water idle, wrinkling occasionally in the sporadic breeze that kept the day from being annoyingly warm. Yesterday, up toward Raton, where she emerges from the mountains, she was an exemplary sunken river across the plain, just the tops of the cottonwoods visible from afar.

And those Chinese explorers, moving slowly down through the Sangre de Cristos ... *Pale Ink* is based on a study of two Chinese texts, texts considered to be among the Classics, regarding mysterious journeys "across the Great Eastern sea." The earliest dates from about 2250 B.C. Known as the "Shan Hai King," it is an account of travels by a fellow named Yu, in the service of the emperor Shun. The author Mertz has painstakingly traced the various routes described in Book IV and believes she has matched several of them with North American topographical fea- tures. Working with poetically limned landmarks, the care- fully noted mileages between them, river systems, and general geology, she has reconstructed, posited, the itiner- aries in considerable detail.

Two of the routes pass through New Mexico. The first (Book IV, section 1) begins on the Sweetwater River in Wyoming—"Shih (Drinkable) River" to the Chinese visi- tors—and moves south via Medicine Bow and Longs Peaks, past Mt. Princeton, the Great Sand Dunes ("much sand" noted by the explorers), and Mt. Blanca, and into New Mexico, where the wanderers described North Truchas Peak (east of Chimayo; "many gems" = turquoise) and Mt. Manzano (south of Albuquerque) before continu- ing south to the Rio Grande.

The second section of Book IV, recounting a separate jour-
ney, begins at the "Mountain of the Empty Mulberry Trees,"
a point Mertz fixes, by the description of surrounding features
in the text, as Hart Mountain, way up in Manitoba. The ani-
mals that resemble striped cattle and make sounds "like a person yawning and stretching" are probably caribou or elk.
Thence south to a peak with many ducks (Moose Mountain,
now a provincial park in Saskatchewan, famous for its water-
fowl) and on into Montana, crossing the Missouri ("much
white-plaster rock"), up the Yellowstone River, through
Wyoming and Colorado (at Medicine Bow Peak they note
with great interest an animal that looks like a rabbit but with
a crow's bill, an owl's eyes, and a serpent's tail, which feigns
sleep at the approach of a man; Mertz nimbly reads it for a
'possum) and New Mexico—Chicoma, South Baldy, Cooks,
and Animas Peaks are attended—and into Mexico proper this
time, almost all the way to Mazatlán ...

Ah, Rip van Winkle. Why not? What a dreamy, pine-
scented, pine-lullabied day.

There are, of course, readers who consider those classic
accounts strictly exercises for the well-heeled courtly imagination.

Not that all those potent mountains and rivers couldn't
hold such a light-footed actual thing.

What a sweet little apple, and what a high, thin-blue sky. ...

Starting back toward the trail I passed a scabby old Osage orange tree hunkering all by itself, still carrying eighteen or twenty fruits, far from Osagiana. Then I climbed back up the road and drove back through Mills (four or five good ruins and the P.O.) and on east through the vast, chaff-colored antelope fields into the town of Clayton to put up for the night.

The next morning at breakfast I realized I hadn't been in Texas for a long time, so afterward I drove the ten miles to the state border and through the village of Texline and just beyond to turn around at Rita Blanca Creek, a grass-taken swale through the plain. Texline, "Home of the Tornadoes."

But the object of the day was highway 406 just east of Clayton, a highly recommended road I had never seen, and a few of its streams and rivers.

Highway 406 cuts north off U.S. 56, eases by a couple of feedlots, then accelerates a notch, up from Bovinia onto higher, loftier ground, the tough roll of absent-minded, sinewy grasslands dear to carrion-peeling raptors. It is a ferruginous hawk stronghold, with accompanying prairie falcons and a skeptical roughleg or two. Through the erstwhile hamlet of Seneca and over erstwhile (or off-duty) Seneca

Creek. Off the left shoulder, Santa Fe Trail (Cimarron Cut-off) landmarks loomed on the skyline, but soon I was down at the first of the streams, the North Canadian River. A dry and stony streambed, but oddly charismatic at that. Still as night. Across the sky I counted fifteen different contrails streaking, melting, smearing, fishtailing hither and yon. With their preposterous silent power and dimension, they very nearly took over the landscape—somehow constrictive, dangerous, and fantastical at once. But then, from up on the south bank, a flock of meadowlarks burst onto the scene—two dozen of them, suddenly milling about, loosing an unfamiliar, aggregate sort of song. A babble or jabber song, a bird guide might term it. I sensed it resulted from the combination of warm late sun and winter gregariousness—of "false spring" and "group psychology"—inspiring a confused but enthusiastic choric inertia. Most all the jabber carried remnants of the eastern meadowlark notes. Obviously happy, they rolled giddily from cedar to cedar across the rocky river-edge hills.

The hamlets of Old Moses and Moses. Off to the north the dark cedars of the Black Mesa began to appear, and gradually I was back into them, the same incremental scattering that marked the approach of Mills Canyon yesterday. Immediately there were more birds. Shrikes, and large numbers of mountain bluebirds, the latter soon everywhere, rocking wide-eyed on the tips of the cedars. When I stopped at the Carrizozo Creek bridge they were still the dominant bird, their windblown flight reflecting their wind-blown calls, while their odd-duck cousin the solitaire tooted in the distance.

Carrizozo canyon is a comfortable place. I dawdled there. That sky, too, crisscrossed by omnidirectional jet trails. The warmth had all the robins muttering. The persistent scolding from the shrubbery turned out to be a pair of brown towhees. And there was a small, perfect grove of youngish cottonwoods, one of those informative ovals of fine line, with the older trees tallest at the core and the steadily younger, slighter generations tailing off toward the edges into knee-high saplings—such a perfect exhibition of procedure, protocol, and order that it illuminated instantly the savvy ancestral sacredness of groves.

And a few moments north, there was the Cimarron running (to exaggerate wildly) from left to right, in a some-what "Anasazi" mode, below an elegant, many-pronged, thin-rimmed mesa on her north. I drove back a dirt road to get a look—90 percent dry; many maps refer to that stretch of the river as the Dry Cimarron—but there was a most interesting handmade bridge across the channel, long sealed off, constructed in an exemplary bricolage of old pipes, metal findings, and rough lumber slabs.

To follow the Cimarron down a ways, east into the Oklahoma panhandle, I put on a Caruso tape I often carry, with the titillating and perhaps hubristic thought that it was a voice new to this road. An anthology of stuff from about 1910, back when Seneca and Mills were thriving communities. The music slowed me down to 30 mph, but after a couple of numbers I realized it was too theatrical for the terrain; too "solo mio" (by which I mean not too lonesome but too solo). Yesterday I discovered that the young Satchmo couldn't stand up on the high plains either—too audience-conscious, too much the lean to flash and please.

So, shortly into Oklahoma, I reached for a tape, "Enuff Said," by a native southern plains group, Sizzortail, and that was just right: many-voiced, nonperfectionist, hymnic without enclosure. Its simple harmony, even when off a degree or two, is its declaration. Proceeding east, I could catch an occasional glimpse of the river a mile to the north. Slowly she rallied more cottonwoods, and by the time I cut north on a gravel road and stopped on her banks to stretch, there was a good-sized grove to look at, with a handsome cut-stone ruin, just a single noncommittal corner of something or other from the precontrail days.

In lieu of a bridge there is a concrete ford across the Cimarron, with runty sunflowers growing out of its cracks. A mossy pool, a few cattails, deep cattle tracks dried in the mud. A big 'coon turd on the cement apron. I occasionally wonder what portion of my life has been spent dawdling like this along streams. In search of turtles, or frogs, or rock bass, or simply lost in thought and basking in the lee of the great iambic-tetrameter noun Inconsequentiality. (And it is exactly like driving, car-dawdling along a dusty back road, craning to see out all the windows and keep up with every skyline.) A set of finely etched Hours like a deck of diminutive hand-colored "Creeks and Rivers" trading cards. At optimistic moments they—those hours—glint as a kind of tortoise-versus-hare karmic pollen-pelf.

I thought the Carrizozo bridge was still, but that Cimarron crossing was stiller. I ate lunch in the warm sun, sitting on the hood of the car. Quiet as a tree ring. Two days before Thanksgiving, and it must have been 60 degrees, again. The bears grumbling on; the roughlegs, just down from the arctic, must have been on the warm side too.

The gravel road would take me thirty miles north, into Colorado and eventually to a highway. From Kiowa to Comanche National Grasslands. That place was so still I finally whistled as loud as I could up- and downstream. Cattle looked up from the willows. Then a raven squawked, off to the south, just as I got in the car.

Swamp Angels

At the end of May, one morning when summer is taking over on the plains and creeping into the foothills, when it is obvious that the spring is past and the warm season is set-ting up, the hermit thrush will come to mind, and we will drive twenty or thirty minutes into the mountains and walk up one of many dependable canyons to listen for its song.

Long Canyon, for one. Into the immediate cool of its shadow and aroma of its pines, through the first streamside popple and up the soft trail. It is a semiformal outing, un-hurried, with regular stops at the bluebells and the rotting log and the big fern brake pouring at one point down the hill, and the single strand of spider filament stretched in-sinuatingly between two young thirty-foot spruces.

For the first third of the hike there are sounds from below. Traffic pulling on the main mountain road and inadvertent thoughts of the decades-old car bodies rusting among the plum thickets at the foot of a steep cliff in a lower canyon, a place where the MacGillivray's warblers will be singing. Then the noise fades and the brash coolness of the canyon is the main thing at hand. There is a sizable stand of hazel, or filbert, beside the upper trail, many of the trunks still bowed from late wet snows. Even appraised without glasses, the bark on the younger, half-inch-through ones has a lovely speckling to it, like the throat of an exotic lily or the skin of some delicate amphibian. Vireos and flycatchers sing from the ponderosas.

And finally, from far on up, a hermit thrush song, from way off on the sunlit tip-top of some aromatic ridge over toward Green Mountain, and we stop beside a drooping apple tree still in blossom in this slow, shady place and sit down on the slope among the larkspur to listen. By the time we are settled, apricot in hand, the bird has stopped. Just a taste; four or five bursts of the distant song are all we got, but they will have to do for now.

Not much for one of the most exalted songs in the bird world—a song often considered the premier avian vocalization on earth. But even at a quarter-mile distance its oddly commanding tone and whirl of cadenza is remarkable as a phenomenon beyond the ordinary.

Nineteenth-century writers loved to praise it. The "ineffable charm and sweetness," suggesting "a serene religious beatitude as no other sound in nature does," its "peace and deep solemn joy that only the finest souls may know." The "bursting of a musical rocket" and the silver tones as of "the oboe superadded to the flute."

F. Schuyler Mathews rose about 1900 to defend the hermit against the nightingale, the European challenger sung by everyone of clout from Shakespeare through Byron to Matthew Arnold: "The song of the hermit thrush is the grand climax of all bird music; it is unquestionably so far removed from all the rest of the wild-wood singers' accomplishments that vaunted comparisons are invidious and wholly out of place." After six or eight pages elaborating upon and illustrating the thrush's range and brilliance, Mathews wraps up the once-heated North Atlantic controversy swiftly and cleanly—"There is no score of the nightingale which can compare."

And suddenly the realization that most springs eight or ten snatches of distant hermit song are all we can manage and thoughts of the near-at-hand, confidential parts of the music we have been missing from afar (one turn-of-the-twentieth-century naturalist claimed you must be within thirty yards to get it all) settle in as an alarming deficiency.

Thrushes and their songs have always been emblematic of secretive beauty from the shadows, haunting voices from remote lairs. "Swamp angels" they used to call both the hermit and the wood thrush. So distant, so secretive, subject to such speculation that Audubon, for example, declared with confidence, "The Hermit Thrush has no song." And by their inner/upper forest natures their songs are usually witnessed in contemplative and solitary surroundings during the most reflective times of day.

The wood thrush is usually the only singer allowed even near the hermit in the rankings—the "vocal expression of the mystery of the universe," "the harmonious tinkling of crystal wine glasses combined with the *vox angelica* stop of the cathedral organ"—and if for me it stands alone as the orchestrator of high-pensive song it is no doubt because I have stopped to listen to many dozens of them in various deep woodlands east of the Mississippi and often instinctively turned and made my way quietly toward the bird for a closer audience, and because its notes conjure an associational scale running from heartbreaking blanket brevity to the purest prismatic exultation.

The Swainson's thrushes are first-rate society when they move through town in May and stay a while, sometimes a full week in the yard, lying low in the dark of the shrubbery and singing their lovely, hard-to-place songs at first light and at the gloaming.

But the recurring realization that I was missing perhaps the subtle best of the hermit's song made me uneasy, incited

a new craving for thrush song in general, and two weeks
after going up Long Canyon I drove up to the Medicine Bow
mountains in southern Wyoming, to a place I remembered
the veeries frequented, to see if they were there. ...

West from Laramie, through some of the least thrushlike
habitat imaginable—dry plains in a dry year—keeping an
eye on the heights of the Snowy Range ahead, also un-
thrushlike ... but somewhere in between there will be cool,
dark, willowy streams where the veeries will be waiting; a
first glimpse of the Little Laramie River soon sets the tone.

I camp on the west side of the range at about eight thousand feet, a campsite in a pleasant meadow with scattered
pines and aspens and the saskatoons in flower, setting up
the tent in about the same spot as twenty years ago, close
to the stream and its aspen and willow stands, and sit down
to wait, essentially, for sundown. Kinglets and Audubon's
warblers feed in the spruces. Siskins, and a goshawk, and
moose tracks over across the fence by the river.

I gaze at the fifty-foot spruce snag nearby long enough
to think how nice it is that trees get to stand around for a
few years after they're dead, and finally, after a ham sandwich and half a bottle of zinfandel, about 8:45, the first
veery sings from beyond the stream; then perhaps three

others quickly join in. The songs are brief, almost clipped renditions—the evening is quite cool—and they go on for only five minutes. Then, again, eight or ten minutes later, by which time I am deep in the sleeping bag, but listening hard.

At ten minutes of five the next morning a single bird begins singing at the first possible lighting of the eastern sky. Now the song is more extended, the glass-harp roll of the delivery more firm. I crawl out of the tent, climb the log fence, and walk over into a small aspen stand to listen. The other veeries eventually start up, and the morning is in order. (One of the old-timers wrote, back East, that to experience the veery to the utmost you must hear them completely alone.) The song is as they say: silvery, ethereal glissando. ... Like lively stream water resembling red chert. ... As delicate as the saskatoon flowers.

By the time the sky is anything approaching blue, the thrushes are quiet for the day. There is a true frost on the car windows, and the binoculars are almost too cold to handle as I wait for the water to boil. Even such a cosmopolitan birdman as Roger Tory Peterson once commented on the perpetual near surprise and elemental gratitude upon finding a species *there* when you go out in search of it. But there they were, the willow thrushes as they were once known, still there in their little colony along the roaring of the mountain stream.

At a certain age, it is not so difficult to imagine a decision to gauge the accumulative valence of one's being by the number of moments passed near singing thrushes, as well as with cheeses of character and beside the breaking of surf. ...

The wood thrush song's elegiac beauty rests in some good part on its form, its unearthly patience and pacing, on the steadfastness of the simple variations.

As the key to the hermit's brilliance lies in the remarkable formality of its structure—the opening single note, the setting of the stage—and then the almost casual, heroic toss-off and virtuoso world-weariness of its bright finale.

Each year it is a further test of metaphor. ...

Both the hermit and the veery induce a smile, while the wood thrush can make you slowly shake your marveling head.

The veeries usually have the asset of multitudes. And the pent-up, sudden frankness of their quicksilver song is stirring in a way I think of, this early morning, as Medicine Bow Garboesque.

The Mississippi to Hannibal

for John Deason

I've crossed the Mississippi many times in a near-casual manner, by car or by bus or by train, followed it briefly on occasion. I took a short boat ride on it once, and saw from a passenger jet one daybreak the miles of great oxbows below St. Louis throwing a brilliant daybreak orange. Always a remarkable feature, of course—one morning an Amtrak porter walked the aisle as the eastbound Zephyr started over the bridge: "The ri-vaire ... the ri-vaire"—but somehow never truly anticipated as much as it might seem to deserve.

This time, having opportunity to accompany it for a few days, I felt a need to start the occasion in a more formal way, to approach the river in more cognizant fashion, and to look at it in a slightly more organized way—if nothing more, then as a stubborn adherent to the theory that the poetical, as Plato suggested for the political, is not cumulative, is not automatically transmitted from generation to generation; that each new wave must learn anew and look again at the world, its own cup to fill.

So from the southwestern quadrant of Wisconsin, the seat of my mother's people—I could live a few decades there just on behalf of the names: Hazel Green, Beetown, Blue Mounds, Spring Green, Sun Prairie—I decided to gain the Mississippi in the sensible way, via the sensible tributaries, and drove over to pick up the Kickapoo River near the village of Viola, then turned downstream. Down the narrow valley through modest wooded hills just coming into April leafage. Down through Readstown and south, close to the river's steady journeyman flow, where the ridges gradually lengthen and lift. Through Soldiers Grove and holstein meadows, cornfields and calendaresque red barns, and into the apple country around Gays Mills, then the Petersburg flats, the river wider but still smooth and sensible. A warm, pleasant morning with the redbirds singing and spring peepers pounding from the lowlands.

Below Steuben, the road leaves the Kickapoo and climbs high above for immense vistas of the lower valley. Moments later I was on the Wisconsin River, a mile or so upstream from where the Kickapoo joins it, and moving southwesterly down that broad, swamp-wet valley on highway 60, a significantly larger road on a significantly larger stream, the approach gaining explicitly in scale and implication as I continued slowly down and into the town of Prairie du Chien, and finally to the edge of the big river itself.

Friends had suggested that I stop at the Reno Bottoms, just north of the Iowa-Minnesota line, for a taste of what they called the "old river," a place where a sizable dogleg of a levee has preserved a few miles of swampy, change-able bottomland reminiscent of the river edges before all the dams went in.

I drove there the next morning, along the Iowa bluffs with their fingerling birches. Across the river their Wis-consin counterparts lay blue-gray, moody and taut, arch as the Adirondacks or a Labrador range. I parked at the Reno Bottoms boat launch and walked out the levee to the spill-way, dry at the moment. The channel of the "old river," from that vantage point, appeared to be some forty yards wide, edged on either side by the dense maze of sloughs, backwaters, and paddies, lagoons and stump fields amid the forest, and countless brief, linear islands one tree wide that is the signature of the old flow. Hooded mergansers watched from behind a log jam.

Then I went on out—some high school boys were fish-ing from the upstream levee bank—to where the dogleg cut

90 degrees downstream, and walked south. It was a classic introduction to the early-twenty-first-century river. On my right a considerable stretch of the pre-lock-and-dam creature—mature, thick-laced woodland with mallards in its puddles and a bald eagle in its trees, swamp white oak sloughs, osier, and deep leaf-pudding. To the left, the new river. Smooth, steely gray, monocultural. Small rafts of bluebills and goldeneyes at rest in midflow, and skeins of the same moving low above the surface. Farther on, a big flock of coots was feeding near the levee shore. Unhunted birds in this era, they were far less skittish than the scaup or the mallards, but even so the entire quarter-mile-long collective organism of them drifted subtly a few inches farther from shore as I passed.

The new river is wide there, but I was near enough the Wisconsin shore to make out the waves striking the base of the bluffs, lapping against them in what struck me as a somehow unnatural and intrusive manner, and for the first time I felt a tremor of the new Mississippi, even that far up, as something suggesting a lake. When I swept the middle of the river through binoculars I realized it was quite full of ducks, diving ducks. To the north the bluffs stepped off, remarkably even, smoky-gray and bushy-headed.

After a while I returned to the car, looking right, left, right—starting to get the drift of it all. The fisherboys had departed, and large redwing colonies in the old river tangles were leading the April charge.

I had been walking slowly and driving slowly all morning, looking and looking at the river, trying to gain a hold as much as anyone onshore can gain a hold. It was slippery in the mind and eye, as difficult to grasp as twentieth-century Walden Pond or something like the Humboldt Current, and to write even these quick notes about it left me shy.

I remember driving over it on the Interstate 80 bridge, very slowly, gingerly, during the great flood of 1993. I remember reading certain boy-level, pelt-and-crucifix histories of the upper heartland where the river set the essential rules. And group chant-spellings of the wonderful name in fourth-grade classrooms. I wrote a poem-line when I was twenty-one: "Say Mississippi sometimes/and the eyes close." But all the same ...

It was easier from a high place, like the bluffs among the effigy mounds, back down in Iowa. From there you can see it as the potent, patient, viscous organism that it is.

I climbed the long hill and walked out through the mounds on top and found a place to sit not far from the

Great Bear effigy. A sturdy April breeze had the oaks and grapevines swaying. Through the leafless forest the river, its various channels, a chilly April blue. A barge moved up-stream. Across the way and just below, the long-standing village of Prairie du Chien again.

The mound groupings comprising the national monument extend some three miles along the blufftops, above and below the mouth of the Yellow River. (Given the attention devoted to the place, I couldn't help thinking the mound builders had a more evocative name for the stream than "Yellow.") Repre-sentations of bears and soaring birds are accompanied by var-ious lapidary arrangements of small, distinguished conical and elongate mounds. The bears were composed, some 1,500 or 2,000 years ago, in the simplest of cookie-cutter profiles. Yet so oddly true—they capture the mind-free slackness and ease of a mammal—think of an English sheepdog—asleep on its side. The birds suggest troupes of giant, graceful, wing-locked swifts. And even, or especially, the recurrent "boulevards" of the unassuming conical mounds, their careful intervals, evoke a reverence and an attention on a more abstract plane and add a metaphysic worthy of the vista.

A reverence of great poise. Reverence for a place and all its conditions, a place with a big river in it and a sky above. Even a river god, perhaps, but one without the lurid, superstitious

disfigurement of the banks of the Ganges, for example—
even though a pedestrian pilgrimage from the Mississippi's
source to its mouth (and back) in very small, preordained
steps, like the traditional *pradakshina* in India, might be a
blessed passage, and to die on its banks not an ignoble goal,
and the thought that her waters could cleanse the wrong-
headedness of a million births a cheering concept.

I have always admired the principle of giving a great river
gifts of homage, as they do with Mother Ganga, floating
little leaf-boats carrying marigolds or rose petals or a few
drops of morning cream. And the hundreds of metaphori-
cal praising names for her in the Sanskrit texts: Fear
Chaser, Lovely Limbed, the Milk White, the Having the
Appearance of the Sacred Syllable *Om*. But then, those
sages were far along, considered *any* confluence of streams
a sacred place. ...

These earthworks are quieter. And high above. The
April breeze nips. The bears—the Great Bears, the Little
Bears, the Marching Bears—are done just right, have the
quintessential lines of constellations on a star map.

From Prairie du Chien I crossed again in the early morning back to the Iowa side and started south on the Great

River Road. After an hour, there was the Turkey River easing in from the west, and I took the gravel road down it, looking for more mounds, the Turkey River Mound Preserve indicated on one of the maps. I drove in three or four miles, down to the edge of the Mississippi. There was no sign of mounds, so I turned around. Seen from the Mississippi bottoms, the ridge-bluff I had just passed below culminates in a narrow, rocky point much resembling the Flatiron Building. I drove back up the Turkey road and stopped to consult a solo fisherman near at hand. He said the mounds were set atop the ridge above us, but there was no ready access to the heights by foot or car.

He was a friendly man, a native of the area who had re-cently returned after years of working elsewhere. He had a folding chair and a large plastic bucket full of gorgeous red horse suckers, six or eight of them brilliant in the sun, each a foot and a half long. He said he cuts them up crosswise and his wife "cold packs" them—salts and spices and cures them in mason jars. In a matter of weeks they taste like salmon.

I went back down to the ferry landing on the Mississippi just below the mouth of the Turkey. The ferry crosses, summers only, to Cassville, Wisconsin. Ten dollars for a car, one for a walker. There is a big, hyper-real coal plant on the opposite shore. A tug was moving a dozen barges plus a Minnesota Centennial Showboat upriver while a long freight train rolled south across the way. Some fifty miles upstream on the Turkey, in the 1890s, Antonin Dvorak walked the river woods near Spillville, hearing the American birds. A local scarlet tanager made it into a passage in the Quartet No. 12, opus 96.

Thinking, as I continued south, of those jars of red horse on a dark shelf, that Turkey River specialty, reminded me of another modest delicacy I found at a salad bar in Prairie du Chien the other night: pickled chicken gizzards, next to the tart beets and the corn relish and just preceding the catfish platter.

I stopped at Breitbach's Inn in Balltown, Iowa, a place that has served food for a century and a half, and bought a piece of fresh, sticky English walnut pie, to go.

On the booming hilltops south from Turkey River stand many nineteenth-century farmhouses, on the very heights, overlooking miles of the Mississippi and its valley, family places that have seen the river day after day and year after year, comprising the durable second rung of the partakers, following only those who ply it, touch it heron-wise.

Down near Sageville I went over to check the flow again, got out between the railroad tracks and a massive John Deere plant. There were five canvasbacks, eight bluebills, and a couple of grebes near shore, and a lapdog barked from a nearby trailer. The river full. Even vat-like.

I returned to the highway and went straight to the Little Maquoketa mound site, whose signs I had noticed coming in. There is a handy trail up to the ridgetop. Bloodroots were blooming. The peepers were audible from the wet-lands below. The works here consist of a simple elegant grouping of thirty-two conical and oblong mounds dating from the first millennium. As always, they follow the line of the ridge, punctuate it in the most unobtrusive rhythm, and as always it was a restorative pleasure to stand beside them, their modest presence and progression suggesting the bumps of a backbone, familiar, even mildly erotic in its aesthetic offhandedness and its mock lassitude among the quiet oncoming vernal mix of oak and hickory.

At the ultimate mound, a large dead bole had fallen, smashing down the chain-link fence protecting the works. It was an entrance, and from the "prow" of the mound I could catch a glimpse of the gray Mississippi a couple of miles to the east, just a glimpse above the roofs of the John Deere complex.

Below Dubuque (where, if memory serves, my uncle Huey Diggins hailed from), more and more the Mississippi presence off to the left is more like an impoundment than a river, and finally even the most minor of tributaries attracts the eye more than the river does, and the towns, the bricky old towns like Bellevue, are more interesting, with their weighty old taverns and hotels and butcher shops. At lunch in Sabula, a village set on a river island, one old man called across the room to another, every minute or two, "Have you turned over your rain gauge yet?" I crossed from there into Illinois and went south along that shore. The bottom lay wide and agricultural, the bluffs distant. The last couple of days the mounds had been saving the river, giving the trip what tone it held.

Those handsome red horse in the bucket kept coming to mind. Something from an eighteenth-century still life. *Moxostoma*—"sucking mouth." I read later, while looking at Joseph Tomelleri's wonderful depictions in *Fishes of the Central United States*, that the first wave of European settlers found the Mississippi tributaries in that part of the country full of such fish during their spring spawning run, and for a primitive moment Illinois was known as the Sucker State.

By the time one reaches the northern edge of the Quad Cities, the riverbanks are utterly residential, groomed right to the edge of the water, and coots preen daintily on the golf course–style grass.

At Muscatine I rested a few days with friends, looked out at the river from their windows and listened to their red-birds sing. I had forgotten how predominant grackles are in the Mississippi valley, their black vectors and hunkered forms everywhere in yard and village, their calls a con-stant. Even the mourning doves' song sounded different, more languorous and expressive than that of doves farther to the west.

We spent a morning looking around in an old pearl-button factory in downtown Muscatine, several floors of dark and dusty long-shut-down working stations where women and girls about 1900 cut out and drilled some mil-lions of the things, working under goosenecked lamps at their belted saws and drills. The freshwater clams they cut from were of course right out of the Mississippi across the street—burlap sacks of them—and overflowing pails of the

buttons themselves still stood in the entropic corners amid
the spider webs and the squab skulls. A stunning, hushed
blend of primal material and discarded twentieth-century
technology.

Then we drove south of town for a picnic on the levee
(shell scraps from the various buttonworks are a common
levee-fill substance in the Muscatine area), a picnic with
local menudo, and what looked like an empty river, when
swept with the glasses—lest we forget—held great numbers of buffleheads and ruddy ducks far out in the middle.

South from Muscatine and back to the mounds, the set of
low Hopewell works at Toolesboro, gentle cones built on
the wooded promontory between the Mississippi and the
final mile or so of the Iowa River. On a good day you can
stand at the edge and inhale, from the bottomlands below,
a scent-mix embracing all four seasons from a stack of
many years. A pretty place with phoebes calling and the
mayapples just unfolding, where you read of "bird men
with weeping eyes" (a now rare regional motif).

Marquette and Joliet, descending the Mississippi in
1673, commented on the stands of large cottonwoods
along this stretch of the river. The locals, Peoria people of

the Illinois nation, made fifty-foot dugouts from the trunks. In those fluid days, the big river was called the "Ohio" by the Iroquois back East and the "Mississippi" by Algonquians (and the French in the upper valley), and the Ohio was known to many as the "Wabash." The Peorias served the travelers a feast of many courses: cornmeal mush flavored with marrow fat, then fish, dog, buffalo, and "excellent watermelon."

I dropped across the muddy Iowa and south through broad, hypercultivated flats. But route 99, the Great River Road, mercifully hugs the sycamore hill-bluffs on the western edge of the valley. Daffodils bloomed in the farmyards. I crossed back into Illinois at Fort Madison, seeking a smaller highway, and south through last fall's corn stubble. A dead woodchuck. The west wind had the fat river lapping near the road's berm. An occasional weather-blistered duck blind offshore bobbed in the steady chop.

I crossed again in a short while, into Keokuk, Iowa, and through the tired old downtown, worn brick stores, and the sooty Hotel Iowa ("Fireproof"). It was hot in Keokuk, probably in the mid-80s, and looked like full summer in a border state. Toddlers in swaddling clothes staggered on the dandelion-dotted lawns. I decided to stop for a breather and followed the signs to the Keokuk National Cemetery, a cool reserve of steep hills and gullies with generous oaks and many hundreds of the standard-issue white military gravestones where Iowa sergeants and their wives rest in the shade, and I rested in the shade.

And then south, over the wide, muddy mouth of the Des Moines (a variant early name for the red horse was the Des Moines plunger), and across the flattest-yet Mississippi floor and into Missouri and down big, busy highway 61 to Hannibal.

The Mississippi changes at Hannibal, the river in my head, at any rate, and perhaps in a few other international imaginations. Thanks in good part to the work of Mr. Twain.

To the north, upstream, the river is largely uncaptured in any major associational way by either literary claim and setting or widespread myth. Hereabouts, Twain's peopling of the river and its islands and banks changed the central Mississippi the way Civil War action just to the south and the blues men way on down, and then New Orleans, and then the Frankensteinian load of chemical fertilizer runoff blasting into the Gulf qualified and colored those reaches and shores.

To the north it is a free-flow stream, in the realm of the imagination if not of the literal. The great mounds and the long beauty of its bluffs and hazes compete with a shadowy, rawer legacy of a river dominated over recent centuries by a two-fisted commerce and in the collective mind as a strictly-business demarcation for surveyors and the guvnor in general. The fishermen know better. But Keokuk, the Sauk who sold most everything, the Keokuk syndrome, surfaces at moments as representative of that cachet, that squirmy, official side of the river.

From the Black Hawk Purchase Treaty of September 1832: "Accordingly, the confederated tribes of Sacs and Foxes hereby cede to the United States forever all the lands ... to wit: Beginning at the Mississippi River at the point established by the Treaty of Prairie du Chien ... thence up to a point 50 miles from the Mississippi ... thence in a right line to the nearest point on the Red Cedar of the Ioway ... 40 miles from the Mississippi ... and by the western shore of said river to the place of beginning. ..." The river as a bodiless, legalistic *line*. And Keokuk, "He who has been everywhere" or "The one who goes about alert," who traded away most everything, now has a monument in the town bearing his name. But in his final years, after the Sauks had drifted listlessly into northeastern Kansas, even his own clansmen would not look him in the eye.

Twain's treatment of the river changed that, locally and beyond, changed it as the locks and dams would later, brought the Mississippi as a creature from the realm of the plat book into the realm of neighborhood, ally and accomplice, and the uncompromising affection of summertime boys. His "A river without islands is like a woman without hair" connects handily to "If the river was whiskey and I was a divin' duck. ..."

Accordingly, I at one time entertained strong notions about Hannibal. Stopped there often while driving one way or the other, and thought of it as a charmed or favored town in a good place, much the same way I would think of the long-gone Woodland or Fox villages along the murky Mississippi tributaries—the Turkey, the Maquoketa, the Skunk, the Ioway. ...

One day, years back, there was a prothonotary warbler singing from a telephone wire near the railroad bridge just south of the main landing—a favored town. Another morning, after staying at the Tom 'n' Huck Motel, I happened across Virginia's Place, on Bird Street, about a block from the Clemens' home, an old-time restaurant of the dying-breed sort that occupied the ground floor of a stubby,

beet-red, two-story building I would venture was a contemporary of some of the mid-nineteenth-century Twain-
related structures in the neighborhood.

The food was good and local. The gravy on top of the
biscuits had shooter-marble-sized chunks of sausage in it.
But they had just posted the upcoming lunch specials, and
that changed the shape of the day. There would be ham and
navy beans, liver and gravy, and a beef and macaroni platter, all in the three-dollar range. But it was the carp sandwich that caught my eye. In a few minutes I decided I
would wait around town until 10:30, when the specials
would be ready.

I had three hours to kill. As I suspected, Hannibal
proved to be a perfect place to idle, loiter, and generally
while away. Not only possessing the great Tom Sawyer
precedent of lush daydreams to be traced in the dust with
the big toe, the waterfront part of the town is small enough
to avoid confusion and riverine enough to have an engaging texture.

I wandered down to the river and spent a few moments
trying in vain to estimate the width of the Mississippi and
watching a family of terns maneuver offshore. I found a pair
of catfishermen setting up on the breakwater, fine-tuning
their sinkers and their big radio.

Then I took a stroll south via the railroad tracks, over a small creek and through a backside tangle of weeds and heavily fruited mulberry trees and flood detritus and rotting old riverfront buildings, and went back to the landing via the boarded-up Mark Twain Hotel, and sat down to watch the river traffic. Pretty soon a tug appeared, pushing barges upstream. It was the *Prairie State*, and the cargo was grain, piled high and covered with tarps. Half a dozen grackles saw it coming and flew out to join it in midriver for a quick snack.

I leaned back against a big rock and half dozed in the sun for a while, then walked up toward town. I read the small marker in memory of Jake "Eagle Eye" Beckley, a Hannibal boy and Hall of Famer, first baseman for a number of National League teams at the turn of the twentieth century. I noticed an ad for a twelve-pack sale on Jax beer, a New Orleans specialty and solid evidence of the river as culture-carrying artery, and went down the alley to the Becky Thatcher Bookstore. In Mark Twain's *Autobiography* I found on page 4 a heroic one-hundred-word catalog of rural Missouri foods, lovingly braised in the memory, ranging from fried chicken and roast pig to succotash and peach cobbler. It was 10:25. With an easy pace I would be at Virginia's right on time.

I had never had the opportunity to eat carp or other "rough fish," though I'd read glowing English accounts and had met people who in their formative years were exposed to such silty-water delicacies as fried gar balls. So that morning, for $1.45, I was served a handsome, huge carp sandwich composed of three fillets rolled in cornmeal and fried crisp, accompanied by white bread cut on the diagonal, with sliced onion, tomato, lettuce, and tartar sauce. I remember wishing I could see the river while I ate, but that was youthful whimsy. The fish was mostly sweet and good. At stronger moments it was wise, instinct informed me, to add more onion. But mostly sweet and good. ... There wasn't leisure to wait around all day to see what was coming up for dinner, so I walked off and left town happy.

That was almost twenty years ago. Virginia's site is now occupied by an uninteresting repaneled diner; but the Mark Twain Hotel is still standing, still idle. It was a Sunday afternoon this time through Hannibal, and I took a shorter walk down to the river. The ri-vaire. Just a few strollers and lollers and one speedboat slapping downstream.

I have never known what to make of the long-running controversy over whether the Mississippi itself or the Missouri River is indeed the main channel of the great system.

Many official measurements use the latter (which makes it some 3,900 river miles from head to mouth, as opposed to 2,500 starting at Lake Itasca, Minnesota).

After five and a half days the Mississippi is a somewhat firmer entity for me, the shore-gazer. Its untouchable midriver flocks, its April odor, its torsion, and its night-squawks. The great name hisses on.

But just then, on the favored Hannibal landing, I remembered a certain stretch of the upper Missouri, its cottonwood groves up there through the old Dakota Mandan country, and got in my car to head west, where I would cross it, give it a look and a nod, at St. Joe in a short half day.

Blackcaps in the Fall

There is a foothills canyon near town where we go each year to pick feral apples. In the half mile of canyon stream bottom above the parking place are at least twenty apple trees that bear respectable fruit. Some are distinctly old specimens of solid Currier and Ives bearing. The lesser trees of indeterminate age are often ratty, many-trunked creatures struggling to hang on in a tough canyon crowded with willows and hazel, chokecherry and bush maple. But the fruit is consistently sweet and often abundant for anyone caring to wade through the brush and poison ivy to gather it in.

I came up this morning to pick a few apples. A cool, well-lit, end-of-September morning with mist hanging over the town and the plains to the east. Some of the apple trees along the grassy trail are already finished, the few remaining apples turning black on the limbs. But others are still laden with fruit. It has been a generous autumn, as the amount of bear droppings below each and every apple tree attests—hand-sized, cider-orange splatters bearing seeds of various wild fruits. There is more and more of it the farther upcanyon I get. It makes the ears perk up and inspires one to whistle a random tune. Less cider-orange than the very color of pomace, or "pomy," as the old timers call it, the aromatic dregs from the cider presses.

After picking a dozen apples from a favorite tree I sit down on a boulder to eat one, or two. Not more than a couple of inches in diameter, frosty damp, about 40 degrees, with a crackle and burst of cold sweetness that almost hurts the teeth. The mellow, transformed sugar of a cordial or a mead. There are a few bees in the persistent asters, and the robins have come up the canyon too, chilly flocks of them busy in the wild grapevines.

One September twenty years ago I joined a friend to pick apples for a couple of weeks in Washington state's Wenatchee valley. A decent apple right from the limb always reminds me of that place, where apple culture is deep and wide. Any time of year up there the dominant artifacts are visible in the various towns: square twenty-bushel apple bins stacked along side streets and eight-foot, three-legged ladders leaning in warehouse yards where trucks back up to docks year-round to take on fruit from the cold rooms.

But from mid-September to mid-October the area booms with harvest and the influx of migrant workers. The task itself is essentially quiet and self-paced. You and a friend or two pick down your assigned rows as you will, filling your waist bags and climbing down to empty them gently into the bin below the tree. Chilly mornings give way to warm afternoons. Babies doze under trees; dogs are picketed at the ends of the rows.

Two or three times a day the owner of the orchard stops by to look over the work, checking for finger bruises on the fruit and apples without stems. Either infraction means that apple will bring a lower price than a picture-perfect specimen. The trick is to palm the fruit and twist it off with a sharp upward motion. It is a simple enough seven-day week, just tiring enough to render you happy in the evening. In those days an average amateur could earn something like $25 a day if he or she didn't spend too much time gazing at the Cascades from the top of the ladder.

The fruit in the Wenatchee country was almost entirely red or golden Delicious then, blunt evidence of the great fading of the old-time apple varieties. They say there were a thousand sorts of apples recognized in North America in 1872; a hundred years later there were perhaps a hundred, most of which were never seen beyond the preservationist orchards where they grew. There must be a small but significant leak in the spiritual reservoir when finely tuned apples

with names like Northern Spy, Wolf River, Cathead,
Fallawater, Blue Pearmain, and the King of Tompkins
County can slip away from an entire continent. The lexi-
con suffers as much as the apple eater.

There were a few small Jonathan stands where we were
picking, near the town of Cashmere, remnants off in a corner of the orchard, but mostly it was a matter of climbing
in and out of the red Delicious trees for eight hours, pock-
eting a few, and going home to the campground via a local
bar, where intense speciation flourished. There were pickers from all over the country: groups of retirees deploying
from Winnebagos; lone clear-eyed backpackers; squads of
obvious professionals; hoboes out from the woods; and rov-
ing little family bands. There was lively talk of pepper picking in California and apricot harvests in Oregon. Some of
the pickers had been in the Wenatchee valley for weeks,
having come early to work the pears. Talk of good trees/bad
trees, big fruit/small fruit. Tall talk of record bins-picked-
per-day. The Mexican contingents seemed to be the perennial champions. Occasionally there was a report on the
local TV news of a pair shattering the old record in a dawn-
to-dusk marathon that drew whistles from the bar crowd.

I remember in particular a sly man in his fifties with a
disorienting squint and a nasty scar completely crossing

his throat. He was a steady, scowling drinker and reminded me of a Disney characterization of "Injun Joe" in
Tom Sawyer. With his twenty-five-year-old son he was
picking sporadically while they waited for a VA check to
be forwarded so they could head for San Diego. They were
natural growling authorities on western American fruit
harvests, they found the local wages insulting, and they
didn't care for apples to boot. They sat low at the bar,
scowling. Every other daybreak on the drive to work we
would see their flimsy old Pontiac broken down in a
slightly different spot on the highway, until finally one day
they disappeared for good.

Hot sun, cool shade, sweet fruit, and mountains around
the edges.

Yesterday morning I sat for a while watching a pair of
Russian olive trees at the edge of an unkempt field. There
were twenty or twenty-five birds in and out of those small
trees, to and from the various seed-bearing weeds nearby.
Yellow-rumps and orange-crowneds, chickadees, white-
crowned and Lincoln's sparrows.

It was, I believe, the first time in my life I'd seen warblers
perching on a wire fence—a milestone the size of a mus-
tard seed.

This morning has a different feel to it. It began colder and has that curious, almost contradictory mix of seasonal elements, with the autumnal aspects on one hand (crisp temperature, mist, apple in hand) and the lean sun, soft pastels, and birdsong of would-be spring on the other (a robin and a solitary vireo in voice up the canyon). There is an ambivalence of proportion, and even of direction.

And after so many Septembers, the crucial distinctions are still to be made, day by day, the sizings to be taken, the details weighed. A driftwood-smooth familiarity accrues over decades, but the specifics-per-morning still demand to be accounted for in relation to predecessor seasons and parallel weeks. Such as blackcaps in the fall ...

Today is a Wilson's warbler day. Blackcaps, as they used to call them. I have seen at least fifteen since I came up the trail. They are a phenomenon not only in the sense of a downsloping flow and equinoctial shift but by their behavior as well. I can think of no other bird whose personality in autumn is quite so distinct and different—more engaging—than it is in spring. In May the blackcaps are businesslike, even quiet, as they return to the foothills. But in September they are an inspired presence, endlessly active, acrobatic, full of aerial pirouettes and hovers, and their signature free falls. Even their plumage seems richer, their bright black eyes brighter.

Many fall mornings in Colorado, Wilson's will be the only warbler you will find. Yet you sense that the entire canyon, the entire watershed, the entire eastern slope of the Rocky Mountains is full of blackcaps and, for the moment, little else. And that is a good apple-time image to hold in the mind as you pause and consider them, their jaunty autumn-blooming nonchalance accompanied by a slightly diluted solitaire song and a slow cricket off below. Coming downstream, down the mountain to anchor the aggregate, twitching and *chic*king, they speak a familiar but elusive dialect, carry an altered, inflected version of the world since last we met.

Prairie Proper

for D. W. Frayer

I crossed the Missouri into Elwood and drove slowly up
from the floodplain, through the defining wooded hills, and
out onto the Kansas prairie. It is always a fortifying experience to visit that part of the country, if for no other reason
than that it is clear on the eye and in the mind as a distinctive habitat zone. It is an appealing landscape; its subtleties
are accessible, its virtues frank and forthright, and you can
always tell when you are there.

As opposed to more spectral American geographies,
such as, to name one, "the Barrens" of western Kentucky,
a feature long since swallowed and hidden by changes in attention and land use and knowable now largely through intelligent hearsay: Carl Sauer tells us that in the early
nineteenth century the Barrens (also known as "the Penny-
royal") comprised a substantial and well-known grassland,
a gently rolling limestone plain, so named not because it
was barren by any means but because it lacked trees and
the settlers lacked, at that point, the French word "prairie."
Today the region is liberally forested, and to detect a trace

of that secret geography requires a thorough briefing and wishful thought.

But when you enter the prairie zone of eastern Kansas you know it at once. There is an implicit richness and diversity to the region that is absent farther west, on the true short-grass plains, and an openness and reach of vista that is missing not far to the east. Even in March there is a sense—more like an aroma—of vegetative density and flexible fertility where the oak-hickory savannas intermingle and flirt with the tall-grass prairie—prairie proper. It is receptive, pleasing, welcoming country.

It is also a cultural repository–homeland for some of the Prairie tribes, as they came to be known in the nineteenth century, and in the strictest northeastern corner of Kansas you will find (eventually and inevitably remindful of the relict stands of bluestem and Indian grass) outposts, often tiny, settlements of the Iowa, the Sac and Fox, and the Kickapoo, and the many billboards for their respective casinos. But even these groups, excepting the Iowa, are at least second-wave prairie peoples, the original tribes of the region, the Kansa, Missouria, and Otoe, having been elbowed to the south and west in the early 1800s.

I was headed for the town of Lawrence, but the March
morning was welcoming enough that I chose to swing a
little farther west and then cut down through the Potawatomi reservation north of Topeka. The rolling prairie was
still in its winter tones: tawny and russet, with the bronze
of last summer's bluestem. The Potawatomi, too, moved
into the Kansas territory in the 1840s, shouldered down
from the western Great Lakes region, and a major body of
them, the Prairie Band, are still there. Their reserved lands
hold a pleasant ratio of lowland woods and powerful grassy
uplands. They are rich in gullies and runs, and the slow-
moving streams support oaks and sycamores and a few
cedars. From the high points on the back roads you can see
a long way toward Colorado.

I stopped along the quiet gravel roads several times and
walked a little, and at one brushy hedgerow raised a flock
of sparrows. I gradually realized they were mostly Harris
sparrows—seasonal prairie-proper creatures if ever there
were one. (In bird books the Harris sparrow's winter range
is shown on the maps as a compact purple-blue puddle-
pocket centered on Kansas and Oklahoma.) A few were
singing wispy partial songs, warming up for the breeding
grounds near Hudson's Bay.

A moment after, I realized the birds were lurking low in a frowsy fencerow stand of Osage orange—another specifically humid-prairie species, before it was carried and planted coast to coast, with this eastern Kansas standing, as I recall, at the far theoretical northern fringe of its tight original range (shown in the tree guide as a red, shrimp-shaped pool extending from about the Arkansas River down through Oklahoma and into central Texas). A signature bird in the signature tree: endemics consorting. It struck me as an elevated conjunction, a quiet, coded moment when a landscape system glints with something approaching semaphore as two of its salients align, as heavenly bodies sometimes align, and glimmer with ancient mutuality and good cause.

I stopped at the bustling Harrah's Prairie Band Casino for a look at the black-velvet, night-for-day interior and to use a bathroom, then continued on to Lawrence.

In Lawrence that week there were more Harris sparrows in the municipal tangles, and the underestimated daily brilliance of the female cardinals, and a few wintering myrtle warblers. ...

But one morning three of us took a ride to the east of town to investigate a weekly auction near the village of

Perry. A family named Gottstein runs the thing. It sets up in an ample farmyard between a large barn and a throw of outbuildings on the broad, pampered prairie flats of the Kansas River bottom: vast dormant cornfields, an occasional swatch of bluestem along the ditches and waving near stop signs, and the latent richness of gardens-to-come, morels-to-be in the distant river trees, future black- and elderberry pies in the making. Every quarter hour a hundred-car freight train rumbles up or down the valley.

The auction was simple and self-contained as any true bazaar. People had brought chickens, ducks, rabbits in their cages. Farm implements and household items. Wire, folding chairs, storm windows, and many greasy boxes of catch-all odds and ends, through which lanky old farmers, old-timers, in overalls carefully pawed. You could buy coffee and donuts at a table over by the barn. One old fellow had brought in a pathetic double handful of finger-sized twigs he had no doubt gathered from his lawn early that morning, and waited half sheepishly to get it up for sale as "kindling."

The auctioneer who started things off was a smooth-voiced man called "Bood." He began at one corner of the grounds and proceeded, item by item, down the irregular rows, calling for bids in the usual auctioneer manner that is always noteworthy in an ethnological way: a semiformal convention suspending ordinary communication for a few moments and inciting a kind of standardized behavior and response. I can still remember several small-town auction-eers I heard, often by chance, as a youth, their inciting voices on the otherwise heavy Midwestern summer air.

But after thirty minutes or so, Bood went for breakfast, and a plump middle-aged woman with glasses picked up the microphone and began to work the crowd, and suddenly it was all in a different mode. My friends didn't care for her delivery, found it strident and annoying, but I was caught by it and followed the proceedings for a while just to listen. Her voice and her method were almost shrill and a bit clumsy but carried an urgency and a prepossessing naive energy that Bood had not unleashed. She had a technique that suggested a motorized mantra as she hollered it out again and again. I couldn't say if it consisted of "Let 'er roll, let 'er roll, let 'er roll, let 'er roll," or something like "Okla-homa, Oklahoma, Oklahoma," or other arcane vocables, among the "Got two and a half, got two and a half, got two and a half, where's three? Where's three?" But the counter-point oddity and the eternal fishmonger edge to it seemed all at once to be an essential ingredient of the prairie place; it charged the morning the way a sudden cry of gulls can activate a landscape, rouse it to full life.

And that is how I will remember her, if I remember her, as the flashing gull of the day—the harsh, transactional, circumpolar voice of the human hawker, hawking. Ever needful, yet sharp as shell on the morning ear.

As we walked back toward the car we heard her readying, getting set for another round: "Okay now, boys, let's clean house!"

A Clear Day on Plum Island

for Christopher Mattison

The Atlantic when we first saw it from the trail through the
dunes was a strenuous blue that seemed to rear before us as
we came to surf's edge and turned flip-of-the-coin north, and
for perhaps the first time William Carlos Williams's image of
a similar sea swaying "peacefully upon its plantlike stem"
came substantively clear to me. The clouds of early morning
had moved on. The ocean was, though breaking in prolonged
rollers against Massachusetts, "honey-voiced" nonetheless.

A flock of gannets foraged two hundred yards offshore,
swallowing everything whole. A few scattered loons in pale
winter plumage rode the rises, while on the beach amid the
occasional grounded gulls a pod of small plovers scurried
about in tight formation reminiscent of their synchronized
flight. Sand dollars, razor clams amid their strops. Tossed-
up lobster pots, bashed and half buried in sand beneath
their tricolor buoys. The several dark humps on the far skyline Cris said must be Maine.

The loons cast skeptical glances at the land, and we
remembered the fossil-poker proposition that wolves are

actually orcas that opportunistically, one eon, gave up on the sea and walked away inland in search of less slippery fare (an osmotic transformation the Haidas and their Wasco/Seawolf acknowledged long ago). And then the Irish dipper I watched one morning in County Mayo, that striking deep chestnut and white gorget design, and the stoat I surprised on a clear morning a week later, atop a stone wall on the Aran Islands, carrying an identical coloration and pattern—and *that* genealogical connection came into focus as well.

We walked for an hour, then turned to backtrack. The ocean sounded different from that direction, the angle with which it broke on the ear. A dozen scoters plying north. To the southeast, in a light shimmer above the blue, Cape Ann, so softly, so calmly named, so near to sea, a far cry from Cape Flattery or Cape Fear. (Those famous footprints found preserved in ash layers in Tanzania, three and a half million years old, three hominid walkers, adults and young, and the famous moment where they obviously paused, turned their attention for a moment to something on the left—a bird of note? or the cry of a bird?—before continuing on their way ...)

The gannets ranged, came and went, seeming to vanish then reemerge ten minutes later through some primal sleight of hand, as the bluefish and the striped-bass schools were no doubt ranging offshore in their prewinter migration from the Bay of Fundy precincts down to Long Island and the Chesapeake. There were good numbers of sizable lobster claws among the beach thatch, and twos and threes of sanderlings paced along the water's edge. Completely at ease with human company, they went about their dainty business within six and eight feet of us, their busy, elderberry eyes sharp but utterly calm, a sophisticated seaside calm—far cries from, say, the wizened, tired-horse eyes of an ibis or the pickerel eyes of a grebe or the shrill hellcat eyes of a rudely interrupted long-eared owl.

Soon it was time to turn inland, back into the sudden muffled hush of the dunes, where the white-throats were singing a gentle pennywhistle song from the dense barrier bush. Yet the October sea followed, and the protocol from that point was of the universal littoral: to seek out the esculent and, with luck, the succulent, to find the nearest *fruits de mer*. As after a day on the California shore, Point Reyes, after the huge flocks of wintering buffleheads on the various inlets, we would end up eating sweet oysters at the barnacled Hog Island picnic table overlooking Tomales Bay, we stopped today in Ipswich, at a place called the White Cap, for lunch. A tacit toast to the erstwhile

Ipswich sparrow (now regarded as a subspecies of the Sa-
vannah), the "Pallid sparrow" of the coastal dunes, first
gunned down and named at the ocean edge of town in
1868. Bowls of chowder, quartered lemons, and a platter
of fried native clams. At the foot of clear Cape Ann.

Timpas Creek

A short time ago I heard mention of Timpas Creek in southern Colorado, probably in the context of the Santa Fe Trail, a reference that included a brief and tantalizing etymology: "Timpas" is Spanish for the stone or plate protecting the top of the opening in a blast furnace through which the molten slag and iron pass into the forehearth. A steely name, compared to some of the eerily isolate rivers of southeastern Colorado—the Huerfano, the River of Souls Lost in Purgatory, the Apishapa ("Stink River").

I drove along the Timpas years ago and still remember both the tough beauty of the land and the summer-mirage elusiveness of the little stream much of the way, tricky enough to even track with certainty that I noted it was exactly the opposite of the Everglades, a river essentially lost and undefinable within the breadth and spread of its flow. But the etymology got me thinking of it anew. The English version of Timpas is, they tell me, "tymp," a word found in Webster's Unabridged but not in the common household version. It spawned the image of a hot, sluggish trickle of saline water oozing over a hot rock on an August afternoon.

And the seed was sown, the name and the thought of the river and the squiggle on the map began to work in my mind, and when a spell of cool weather appeared in mid-June I threw some things in the car and drove off early one morning to check on the Timpas again.

The landscape is always assertive as you approach the Arkansas valley from the north, down through Lincoln and Crowley Counties in eastern Colorado. Gradually the cholla increases, almost as a kind of vegetative boding, almost like the creeping awareness of more and more vultures accumulating in your particular sky. And then you notice, and then ascertain, that although it is very level country you are driving through, it has the unsettling sensation of the horizons resting higher than the center—like the sea, of course. It stirs a vague, deep-seated, tsunami-in-the-wings foreboding.

It gets drier and harsher as you near the Arkansas. You squirm a bit in the seat and double-check your water supply. And the people in the Arkansas valley towns like Rocky Ford, La Junta, Las Animas are friendly enough, and carry on, most obviously, but there is to my eye always a bone-deep quietness in their manner, a rejection after long trial of any sort of energy-wasting expression (either verbal

or facial), a parched-root sort of habitude that has led me
to consider them among the least illusioned people in
North America.

South of the big river it is all more so. Dry, loose-soiled,
sand-saged, sun-struck. Once you get beyond the irrigated
zone bordering the Arkansas the landscape has the look of
semicultivation, suggests a thoroughly resigned culture of
goats-and-cholla. Anything patently human is viewed, in
the end, as dispensable. Rubble piles, tangles of old wire
and rebar, tar buckets, and farm equipment—tossed aside,
simply, at some unknown time, to lie hapless in a dangerous sun.

I stop for a first look at Timpas Creek from the small
bridge on highway 71 some ten miles west of La Junta. It
has a steady, half-muddy flow about twelve feet across.
There is a shaggy willow brake just upstream and the remnants of what must have been a beaver dam. The creek
runs between soft, sand-colored banks three and five feet
high. All told, it strikes me as almost sprightly, given
its name. There is a flock of cliff swallows floating above
the bridge, and from the willows a yellow-breasted chat
whoops and whistles. Old concrete slabs. Scores of rusted
coffee cans.

Continuing south, I can verify the creek by its occasional patch of brush as it wanders through nearly treeless saltbush/grassland. Down where 71 hits 350 there is a Santa Fe Trail marker and an overlook where you may walk gingerly among the needled things and listen for the Cassin's sparrow's song, a delicacy indeed in the harshness of Otero County. It is a sweet, fragile tune, and the little leap of larking flight that accompanies it is almost heartrending given its venue and the vocalizations of its peers: kingbird racket and meadowlark blurts. The Cassin's song, its tenderness, confuses my latent, long-simmering theory that the dramatic differences between the songs of the Eastern pewee and the Western pewee, as between the plumbeous and the blue-headed forms of the solitary vireo, the meadowlarks, and other east-west pairings, boils down to a lack of moisture in the air.

I want to get out beside the stream. Up across from the pale village of Timpas—two dozen shade trees and half a dozen houses—is an accessible bridge where I park and take off across a field along the creek. (I had a brief spell of silliness in which I wondered if anyone might possibly object to my presence.) The stream is fully viable at this point, with long, even swimmable cattail-lined pools at regular intervals. A delicious June breeze bobs in the willows

and tamarisk. The Timpas water is clearer up here, an invit-
ing light green.

Tamarisk, the salt cedar, has established itself as one of
the most common trees in this part of the country. The
Arkansas valley is full of it, as is the Cimarron and dozens
of other southwestern river bottoms. Most of this coloniza-
tion occurred in the second half of the twentieth century,
after the tree escaped from cultivation as an ornamental
both exotic and content in very harsh climates. Its relentless success in this part of the West alarms many people; it
does tend to capture any given habitat to its liking. But out
here, I must admit, it adds a lushness to the landscape and
makes the Timpas pools worthy of sand-sage nymphs and
dryads. Birds seem to love its cover. Up close, its tight
light-pink blossom and scaly leaves suggest a kind of fitting
gila-monster beadwork.

The earth along the stream has a disturbed look to it,
only about half vegetated. Cheat grass, cholla in bloom, a
profusion of some low yellow composite. More of the steady
scattering of rusted tin cans that finally comes to demand
the term "droppings," and every now and then a vigorous
anthill where a coyote has dropped a message of its own.

I drive on, upriver, up the edge of the national grasslands
near the village of Delhi, seeking a stretch of hikable creek

more remote, a little farther even from the harmless highway.
Ten miles above Timpas town, dark cedars begin to show up
on the ridges, taking on a distinctly New Mexican look. The
creek swings lazily, giving forth an occasional tree or bush,
with many hazy, spiny miles visible off to the northwest.

Then there is a series of grand cholla fields, or forests,
all in bright fuchsia flower, as the gradual upstream rise
continues and the uplands roughen. But a few miles above
the ruins of the hamlet of Bloom I realize the Timpas is
"gone." I can spot no trace, no vegetative clue. Gone under-
ground, or dried up, or dispersed and scattered into dozens
of tiny, energy-conserving threads. Only the Santa Fe Railroad tracks carry on as though nothing had happened.

At Delhi I pull into the parking lot of the sole commercial enterprise, the "One Stop" store, to figure things out.
Glassing off to the southwest, I can spy here and there the
odd straggly tree. A mockingbird sings from atop the TV
antenna on the store, sings a perky cholla-country tune. I
can't even tell if the store is still in operation. I drive across
the tracks and take a dirt road to the west. And after three-
quarters of a mile, there is a clump of willows and, sure
enough, a string of shallow pools—it's still a stream after
all, even if it's stalled precariously between the quick and
the dead—even a valiant runt cottonwood.

So I choose a stretch of river on national grasslands property back downstream, across the road from the ruins of Bloom. A dirt track leads to an old ford, where I park, and from there the creek swings north and away from most everything in sight. The breeze is still up and pleasant—it's much cooler afoot than in the car—and the walking is good. A heron rises and flaps south—probably the first disturbance it's had in a good while. And the Timpas is a solid entity again, with plungeable pools beneath sharp fifteen-foot cliffs. There are numerous plants of engaging design that I don't recognize; charismatic plants with, I would hazard, more Nahuatl and Spanish names than English ones.

After forty minutes I drop down onto a small shelf of a valley, a would-be cove where the creek is largely dry stonebed. It is a hospitable place, and I feel I've finally gotten the hang of Rio Timpas. I am apparently far enough away from things that there is no junk on the creek sides, antique or otherwise. A little feeder arroyo cuts in from the west, almost substantial enough for a name of its own. From where I take a seat, cholla looms in silhouette on the jagged bank above. There is a pair of kestrels sailing around the cliff downstream, and then, from the far side of a tamarisk stand, another chat begins to sing. The clump of salt cedar is so dense I doubt he even realizes that I am

here. Like the one at the highway 71 bridge earlier, this
bird's song seems rougher and of more limited vocabulary
than the chats I am used to in the shady foothills. Less
chance for conversation down here, most certainly.

All birds acquire rigorously subjective associations for
people who notice them in any detail. The yellow-breasted
chat has for me a connection strangely moonlit. Ten years
ago a seriously sick friend and I took part in a four-day
healing maneuver on the Pine Ridge reservation in South
Dakota. A Lakota medicine man from over Rosebud way
was running the thing. The two of us were kept relatively
sequestered most of the day, four days in all, and each
evening we would build a large fire down along Wounded
Knee Creek and get the stones heating for the sweat lodge
there. About dark, six or eight of us crawled in, and the
sweating and the singing and praying began. It went on for
several hours, and it was usually midnight or after when
we emerged for good, cleansed through and through, and
there above the summer trees a big moon in a clean sky,
and each time, from the brush up and down the creek,
chats were singing, tooting and chuckling merrily in the
clean moonlight. ... Accordingly, they now carry heavy
freight, probably more of an affective load than many birds
could manage.

As the largest of warblers, chats can sometimes appear almost comical, somehow like a boy who missed a few years of school and stands a foot taller than his classmates. But they are obviously formidable, resilient birds. This Timpas specimen has chosen a galvanized habitat to make its home, and I am sure its handsome south-of-the-border relatives, the red-breasted and the gray-throated chats, are tough enough customers as well.

As I walk off toward the car I can hear the cackling and whistling for a long way. A far cry from the passing-cloud Wounded Knee starlight. From today on I will consider them as, first and foremost, the most durable of their breed, tough as shrikes, tough as Timpas nails, the strongest of warblers, ready for any and all tests of worlds to come.

Going Back in May

I was visiting my hometown in Ohio from New York City. It was a hot July day, a common sort of middlewestern day when the sky is more a glowering white than any shade of blue, and everything shows the bulge of full summer: the fencerows are heavy with bush and tree, the roadsides dense with greenery. Queen Anne's lace and chicory nod in the heat. Pastures and their stands of purple ironweed are hazy. It all has a dusty, hard-traveled look. There is a slackness, a release from the push of spring and early summer, an exhalation after the species work is done.

I wanted to get out and walk, heat or no, so I drove two miles from town and parked along a gravel road and struck off for a sizable woodland where over the decades we had often hiked and hunted. I walked along the edge of a half-grown soybean field, then cut across it toward the woods looming like a dark packed loaf beyond the hot tillage.

In ten minutes I was at the edge of the trees and followed an overgrown sugar-camp road into the immediate cave-cool of the beech-maple shade. I stopped to catch my breath and pull a water bottle from my pack. A red-eyed vireo sang from the dark inner woods.

Then there was another sound, and then a deerfly roared by and came around again. The high autobahn whine from the forest I slowly registered was the sound of many, many mosquitoes and their brethren. The deerflies were suddenly everywhere. I cut for the nearest edge of the woods, and there, just outside, in the shadow of young ash trees, I found a place both out of the sun and away from the insects.

It was a north-facing edge and opened onto simple, somewhat ragged pastureland, a rolling meadow, open knee-high grasses with a midsummer wheaten cast, here and there a patch of white asters or sweet clover, with occasional clumps of blackberry bramble and a fencerow at the far edge with elderberry bushes and sumac along it. A small herd of guernsey cattle grazed lazily; a few of them had moved into the shade of a near-spent old apple tree. A narrow path worn by their plodding angled across and over a knoll. Another black, square woodlot hunkered a half mile to the north.

A field sparrow singing. Dusty milkweed, and the heat-blanched, off-blue sky. A landscape I had known all my life. A herdsman's landscape, utterly different from the strict, stripped horticultural beanfield-terra I had walked across a few minutes before. A "Constable landscape," I suddenly called it. I was almost startled by the recognition. By both my easy, lifelong intimacy with such a scene—my earliest solid memory is a site-specific image of gazing, at age two, through a fence at nearby cattle (guernseys again) grazing beside a country road—and by the remarkable antiquity of the scene, a fundamental composition going back how far? The Middle Ages?

I must have been about thirty years old at the time. I stood there a few minutes gazing, very interested, almost surprised, and almost honored by my circumstantial connection with that continuum and pastoral strain of dailiness and the daddy longlegs cleanness of its lines. The Constable association framed it, of course, gave it a genre, almost a sort of *dialect*. But my antecedents are all of the British Isles, so the bond is far from whimsical.

I suppose it was the first time I realized the depth, the fastness, of the landscape imprint on my own person and saw at the same time the high bucolic stratum of the cordial archetype. It was Ohio, Ohioana, but it was also a brush with a vast phylogeny, and I now assume that it explains in part my casual fondness for the Barbizon painters when I happen across them as well as my long-standing fondness for the music of Henry Purcell.

That Constable zone rides on a sempiternal level, and to
sense it at all is a gift of sorts. But when I return nowadays
to the eastern half of the continent it is in search of more
fine-scaled connection (as the anthropologists might say)
to the landscape and the affective links it holds; it is difficult enough to field and sustain relations of three and four
decades ago, let alone any heat-wrinkled medieval proto-
types. And for the sustenance of such fragile relations it is
prudent to go back in May rather than deep summer. Tem-
perate May with all the richness of those woodlands in
flower, the month of warblers and other delicacies. "The
month of understanding," in Wallace Stevens's words.
That is the time to stroll the old streets and weigh the om-
nivorousness of time and the bewildering disappearance of
so many good, solid things and perfectly innocent people,
and that is when I go back and take to paths and trails
I have known for fifty years. To batten and nourish the
world as it once surely was and to keep alive familiarity with
that realm, those generous broad-leaved trees and the birds
of May, back there, which represent more than any other
aspect the Confucian "one unchanging thing" with which
to counter the ten thousand changing.

Each spring it takes a half day to acclimate, to find foot-
ing in the humid air and the intense surge and canopy of
woods and brush, the humid sky with its vague clouds and
many vultures, the moistness on the skin, the onslaught of
bugs, the ubiquitous scent of honeysuckle. But in an hour
or two the titmouse and the vireo songs take hold and re-
store a deep inner order and reciprocity.

Most mornings I follow a similar route through places I
know the warblers will be: around the small lakes in the
park just east of town, where we used to fish as boys, and
along the clifftop edge of the village cemetery, where we
used to swing from the high, arm-thick grapevines. Four
hours of cool May morning, through trillium and cranes-
bill, finding the warblers always there, but the landscape is
so accordingly keyed, so set within a familial magnetic field,
that an entire other mentality gradually arises, images fil-
tering in as if from the aroma of the honeysuckle, and I can
be watching a blue-headed vireo and thinking simultane-
ously of old Hortense Jenkins in the town of forty years
ago, a bent, almost hunchbacked woman with a dozen cats
roaming her gray house, and her annually dreaded Christmas cookies full of short calico hairs.

Or watching the first rose-breasted grosbeak of the spring
while remembering the giant bur oak in the elementary

schoolyard that I passed beneath each morning and every afternoon, and then the day when old "Deafy" Wright, who worked many years on the village street crew and who could neither hear nor speak, struck into a hornet nest with his scythe and found a sort of roaring voice at last as he raced through the north side of town.

Or a gorgeous tanager overhead, while recalling the folkloric day a pretty girl named Rosie fell head over heels down the junior high stairway in a billowing 1950s skirt (no harm done), and how word spread instantly through the halls that she wore no underthings that particular 1950s morning. ...

Another day I will vary things a little and go up Whetstone Creek a ways before hitting the cemetery, to find a blue-wing up there in the brushy field. On the way I will pass a rotting log, nearly invisible beside the trail, where my father traditionally found morel mushrooms in early May, and will step over to poke about in the wild ginger and Sweet Williams to locate its dwindling form and commemorate *that* May specialty, second only to the warblers, and the heartwarming childish manner in which it takes over the town every year during the season of understanding, sometime in latter April, when you will meet someone on the street or in the store and hear the first morel story of the spring: someone or other, always good with the early spots, found fifty on Wednesday out south of town. This seems unlikely; it's been too cool, you're thinking later that evening, just as a car pulls up outside and the man himself appears at the screen door with a basket of nice-sized mushrooms in his hand and a boyish grin on his face.

It was often less a communal spring-fest than it might sound. People would sooner lose a finger than divulge their prime mushroom territories. I remember in high school being blindfolded, eased into a car by half-serious friends, driven several miles out of town, then spun around a few times before being unwrapped in a moist ash woods near a drowsy creek that I recognized immediately. But I didn't let on; we found a dozen morels and some soggy week-old checks from a tornado-exploded bank in Xenia, a hundred miles south.

There were other good morel woods on properties guarded by ferocious farmers. These called for a straight-forward guerrilla dash across plowed ten-acre fields to reach the woods and hit the mother lodes before the old man could get back there on his tractor.

I remember treading lightly through the woods, my father scanning the moist forest floor for mushrooms while I watched the treetops for birds. Amid the general pleasures, he would sometimes stop at fresh boot tracks to read the sign, or pause at a tuft of red flannel caught on a barbed-wire fence and analyze it in good gumshoe fashion: "That's Burling. I'll bet he's sneaking in through the Bader woods."

On most mornings in the middle of May you can expect to find fifteen warblers, and on one with luck you might find twenty. They are the aerators, and after five days or a week of it, the memory cartoons from the town a mile away are almost too thick, and the fleeting beauties of the day before are nearly as tenuous as the involuntary recollections of yore, and it is necessary at the end of the day to regather them, run through at sleeptime the retinal images of the black-throated green high in the hickory in full morning sun, and the Blackburnian mousing along a horizontal branch eighty feet up in an oak—to regather them and maximize the aesthetics and even to substantiate them as fact, so fleeting were they.

Understanding is in some ways an accession and a joining of hands. And the morning twenty-five years ago when

a cerulean warbler plunged from the beech tops to the dog-
wood beside us and fed there for a speechless blue moment
is there with the Connecticut warbler of the day before yesterday, that single, hard-to-believe, split-second view of it
low in the center of the bog. ... And so is the image of my
mother walking home from work with a bag of groceries in
her arms and a lightly knitted brow, up the long West High
Street hill, and the way Dale Gattshall used to drop semi-
annually out the open window of the schoolroom when the
teacher turned her back, drop the ten feet or so to the
ground and walk back into the building and knock at the
door and stand there with a great triumphant chimpanzee
smile on his face when she opened the door and said,
"Why, Dale!"

Muddy creeks and ramp patches and sycamore warblers in
the sycamores. Entire villages as-you-knew-them inexorably
disappearing from the face of the earth. And the slightly
suspect aroma of skunk cabbage down through the years.

The birds are the fine points, stabilizers, like the seas
and the stars.

A Black Hills Loop

The Black Hills of South Dakota, comprising a relatively compact island unto themselves, have always been a good focal point for prairie drives. Imbued with the venerable and the ceremonial as they have been for centuries, they are a satisfying feature around which to throw a conceptual, aesthetic loop, a conscious automotive encirclement to celebrate spring or fall or any given saint's day.

One June I drove a friend from back East up that way. He wanted to see some unobstructed country and, while we were at it, the white-winged juncos, specialty of the region, birds that nest only in the Black Hills and a few nearby outliers.

North of Cheyenne we cut east across the Chugwater road to angle a bit, pick up some dirt byways, and stop for a look at the mouth of Horse Creek below Torrington, Wyoming. We were well out into the rolling prairie boondocks when we saw ahead of us, zipping out of nowhere, a group of six or eight young men or boys in full camouflage gear, helmets and goggles, each carrying some sort of firearm. They appeared at an organized trot from a willowy crease in the hillside, dashed chop-chop across the highway, and by the time we were even with them had moved off across the grasslands to the south and over a rise in that squadron-at-the-ready jog.

We assumed they were survivalist practitioners, probably of the gaming, paint-ball wars variety, out on playful maneuvers, tracking an "enemy" squad to wage make-believe battle in a craggy arroyo. "Playing cowboy." But the sight of them and their fervent concentration, not to mention the obvious scale of their mission in such a vast theater, got us musing about such pretending, "bang-bang, you're dead" pastimes.

We talked about the contemporary "mountain man" rendezvous in the Rockies, those annual gatherings in suspended-disbelief costumery, badger hats and greasy buckskins and twangy yarns, flint knapping and hatchet throwing, where the Caucasian beadcraft and porcupine quillwork is considered by some to be "better than Indian." And of course, even it can't hold a candle to the work coming out of Germany nowadays.

And the Renaissance Fairs. One summer Saturday I drove wearily into a favorite campground in northeastern Colorado to find it overflowing with two hundred people in sixteenth-century garb, much of it having the look of Cub Scout needlework. They were strolling about self-consciously, strumming cheap lutes or shouldering broomstick halberds.

In one clearing, a couple of ceorls were "swordfighting" in slow, stylized motion with plywood broadswords.

Carl turned it to the West in particular, the fascination with the phony, having seen *The Searchers* a short while before, having stared in disbelief at the preposterous "Comanches" with their ridiculous trappings and the farcical use of Monument Valley landscape. And mentioned a show of paintings on the American West he had visited last winter that illustrated the deep roots of the false commercial image. He estimated that 40 percent of the pictures hung were near nonsensical, rumor-based, dreamed up and distorted by either distance (as in Europe) or romantic notions of exotica and its ready market.

It is a subject much written upon. What is endlessly striking, though, is the extent to which such atomized distraction can in the end come very close to undercutting, eating away, the original referent on which it based its two-dimensional wares, until the entire subject is widely greeted with the wateriest of grins.

There were many things more solid and more pleasant on the landscape as we drove. The discussion simply made us wonder out loud a little about validity, continuum, duration on this vulnerable continent and in the West after the century of "Hollywood" and the great filmic gullibility, and

just what difficult-to-imagine mentality might be afoot in
another fifty years, vaporous fruit of a generation who in-
herited what students of the field call a chronically "simu-
lation-infested" landscape.

We paused near the mouth of Horse Creek on the south
side of the North Platte. By scurrying along some lesser
dirt roads and following the Burlington Northern tracks
you can get in fairly close to the big bottoms where so
many tribes gathered in 1851 to hear the pitch about the
Fort Laramie treaty. We ate lunch and admired the extensive cottonwood groves. Carl had brought an ice chest
with, among other things, four cool over-easy egg sandwiches with a little ketchup, mayonnaise, and very thin
onion.

Then we drove east into Nebraska and up through the
panhandle—swift fox country—down the White River
and into South Dakota, where we jogged out of our way
slightly to stop and see my old friend Emerson Spider on
the Pine Ridge reservation. Emerson was quietly bemoan-
ing the price of peyote buttons coming up from west Texas.
He had recently paid two hundred dollars for a thousand;
a couple or three decades ago the same bagful cost twenty-
five bucks ...

And proceeded north, with the Black Hills now visible
off to the left, past outbreaks of badlands, past the crooked
sign pointing to a small mixed-blood hamlet where a Lakota
holy man with a wonderful name had been accused some
years ago of making scandalous advances toward a visiting
white girl right in the sweat lodge itself—it was the talk of
the region for a few weeks—and up Rapid Creek to stop for
the night near the city thereon and named thereafter.

I fell asleep to lazy visions of other seasons on the plains,
other long loops from river to river and powwow to powwow.
Eagle Butte. Rosebud Fair with its incessant wind and blow-
ing hats and feathers. Two days tented at the woolly, rule-free
gathering at Stand Off on the Blood reserve in lower Alberta.
The pounding of dancers' bells at the Little Shell powwow
high above the Missouri in North Dakota, and the "49"
songs going well after midnight at the Lame Deer Fourth of
July celebration. The sprawl of the Milk River Indian Days
up at Fort Belknap, the smell of the camp in early morning,
waiting for a coffee stand to open. Tiny Red Scaffold, and the
Bullhead "VJ" powwow, way out there on Grand River,
where for years the Hunkpapas reenacted a few bloody moments of the Okinawa fight on a nearby slope. Weeks or ten
days at a time, mortared with drums and song, brazen pit toilets, scrawny dogs and meadowlarks, not a hypester or a
heightener or a stunt man in sight ...

❧

The white-winged junco, besides nesting only in the Black Hills area, is the only bird species that breeds exclusively in the Black Hills uplift. It is a doubly emphatic Black Hills creature, even if it's considered a subspecies, as it currently is.

We drove out early next morning to Bear Butte east of Sturgis and climbed that always restorative trail around the flanks, from aspen into coniferous slopes and Olympian slag and finally the long, aromatic view to the east with its vast river corridors that relieve all human motive and migration of any mystery whatsoever. And there were juncos, some of them showing wingbars—Bear Butte juncos, a specialty within a specialty. And even a moth-pale Krider's redtail, another plains morph, sailed by as we started back down the trail.

Then we drove over into the hills, to Deadwood and Cheyenne Crossing, where we walked a little, but not too much, so as not to lose the motion of the Loop, studied more juncos, watching for wingbars, and out into Wyoming again, where the big spaces made us happy. Mule Creek and Redbird and south.

I told Carl what another friend had related from western Colorado: A sizable "bunch" of Butch Cassidy–gang descendants still lived in a certain ungroomed area out there and

apparently exerted a common-knowledge, tough-customer
sway for miles around—heedless, collar-resistant, thriving
like a half-wild grain.

A few moments later in the green June day, I remembered two other occasions—unexpected, mildly dramatic
occasions of patent presence. In the mid-1980s I worked in
a gallery in Colorado that carried an extensive collection of
Edward Curtis photogravures. One day a woman in her
seventies came in and looked around with great interest.
We began to talk. She possessed a lively, earthy sense of
humor and commented on certain of the Oklahoma scenes
with great knowledge. She placed the Southern Cheyenne
Massaum gathering in one of the shots precisely on the
North Canadian River not far from Canton—she had witnessed one of the last of these "Animal dances" as a child
about 1915—and the sun dance photographed by Curtis
as located near Greenfield, Oklahoma, northeast of town
on a big hill visible from the highway. Before she left she
identified herself as Anne Shadlow, from Oklahoma City,
and the great-granddaughter of Owl Woman, a Cheyenne,
and William Bent (of the long-in-place Bent's Fort family,
most influential in the history of the central plains) via the
union of Edmund Guerrier and Julia Bent. The latter, Mrs.
Shadlow's grandmother, had witnessed as a teenager the in-
famous Sand Creek shoot-down in 1864.

And again—I stopped one day at an Apache reservation in New Mexico, took a quick look in an arts shop in the small village, and chatted for a quarter hour with a well-spoken, not-quite-old woman on duty there. She turned out to be, simply, the great-great-granddaughter of Cochise. ...

It is tricky of late to cut to any sort of chase, though perhaps not quite so tricky as the recent century of popcorn-hypnosis puppetry would have us believe.

"There were actual orchards. There were actual men"—a poet must, it seems, remind us again and again.

Carl and I stopped at a rough-and-ready truck stop near Lusk, a heady sample of its kind, full of hard-eating men and a few of their women, a scene which reopened many of the human mysteries that the view from Bear Butte had instantly dissolved.

A little later, the Black Hills loop now officially closed, we paused at the Featherlegs monument farther south. I had assumed for years, noticing it on the Wyoming maps, that it commemorated a native chief or notable, but it turned out to be a marker to a well-regarded and lovingly named old-time madam who, with her girly girls, kept, for a while there, that far-upper Niobrara country lashed down and snug.

Short Days:
Birds & the Turn of the Year

One becalmed, speculative winter I arranged with a friend to receive the little feeder birds that regularly struck the panes of his large French doors. Each time he heard the unpleasant *ponk* from the next room he retrieved the body, ascertained that it was over, and moved it immediately to the freezer. After three weeks he presented me with a paper bag containing, as I recall, two tree sparrows and two juncoes, which I thawed, plucked, and cleaned one Sunday morning, with a thought to Emile Zola subsisting during a lean spell in Paris on sparrows he trapped on his window ledge. I rubbed the two-inch things with butter and put a tiny sprig of parsley in each cavity—poked it in with my little finger—roasted them in a hot oven for ten or twelve minutes, and had a tiny experimental lunch.

2.

There is sometimes a need in the dark of the year, when you turn the key in the house door and glance over your shoulder, noticing uneasily the night falling at 4:20 in the afternoon, to dream something up, to rally, mount an excursion for the short days, on principle.

You might hastily plan a trip east, out on the grasslands, to look for redpolls down from the arctic. Pack a thermos of coffee and a bag of sandwiches, drive out a hundred miles, work slowly through the vast stands of dead sunflowers along Crow Creek, and hope to discover a few of those catchy birds among the rolling, air-light flocks of goldfinches.

Or drive south to the set of foothills cliffs where rosy finches often winter, forced down from their summer peaks and snowfields. Wait below the rearing red rock slabs at 3 or 4 o'clock for the birds to come in for their early roosts, and think how out of place they seem at five thousand feet, out of form, somehow like watching petrels dance above dry land.

Or maybe someone has found a snowy owl on the plains, and you will rally that excursion, thermos and sandwiches, the hour-and-a-half drive, down the South Platte, then cutting north, off on a dirt road, twenty miles in, into sandy, snow-scalloped country that appears shiftless even to a prairie lover. A right, a left, another right. Old tumbleweeds piled deep against the fences for miles. Dog-eared scraps of a winter-kill calf. Then, up ahead, two cars beside the road, three cars, and half a dozen persons standing beyond the ditch, spotting scopes set up against the sky. And the beautiful owl sits blinking forty yards off on a windmill fence, and the people talk birds quietly, with the Medicine Bow range brilliant on the horizon a hundred miles west, and the fact that the people are there, came out to greet the bird—from the blackish spotting, someone says, it must be a young one—is nearly as good as greeting the bird.

3.

The ultimate heart-of-winter outing—something to flush the spirit and help lubricate the deep-winter pivot—might be the trip up to Georgetown and the twelve slow miles south from there, up past treeline to Guanella Pass, where, at 11,600 feet, you can walk the tundra in search of white-tailed ptarmigans—also "down for the winter"—trying to spot them in their pure white December plumage. They like the streamlined bouldery slopes where a few widely scattered bristlecone pines grow, half covered in drifts, along with low willow shrubs. That is where they spend their winter days, nibbling willow buds or napping in the sun.

If you are lucky enough to be there when the wind is down, it is a memorable place to walk for an hour, crisscrossing the hillsides, watching for sitting birds. Above to the immediate east and west, higher ridges and peaks rise, and the thought that the ptarmigans' finely tuned sensibilities have moved them in due time from their breeding communities *up there* to the slightly less severe tundra swales *down here* is breathtaking in a place already thin of air.

It is cold at Guanella even without wind, and the hiking can be tiring over the rolling breakers of crusted snow that are knee deep or more when you break through; best to follow the routes where pale grass still shows. Cumulus puffs boom over the peaks into sudden view. They seem more earthly-familiar than the landscape near at hand. And, high up on a knob, a wandering coyote trail. Out in search of the ptarmigan? Or just a midnight turn to take in the unobstructed tundra stars?

Even if you never spot a ptarmigan, never lock on to the black eye and black bill against the snow field, their delicate inch-and-a-quarter tracks will be abundant, where they moved from bushtop to bushtop. And in that place, on a midwinter forenoon, that is close to being enough: You have been on their solstice territory, shared their climate, and left a few tracks for a thin midwinter camaraderie.

4.

But in the end it is the hawks, winter hawks, that supply a critical cold-season dailiness and companionship near to home. After the leaves drop, they are there in all weathers, the big, intelligent buteos hunched in the bare trees. Stop most anywhere along a winter road and there will be two, three, or four, visible in various quarters of the newly revealed landscape, watching—the most vigilant and un- biased of witnesses. And the pleasure in seeing a redtail at cold sunset hurrying over the highway toward its roost is a pleasure difficult to define.

Then one day in late November, the dark ones, the black hawks from the far north, are suddenly with us, darker- than-shadow, thumb-shaped silhouettes in the cotton- woods, and they will remain, among the less newsworthy raptors, daily presences till the ides of March.

This morning we were out for a look at a December day along a tried, true path not far from town that manages to

cover a minor creek and several small lakes in the course of
an hour or so. At 8:00 the place was clamped under cold,
low frost-cloud. There was hoar on the teasel, and we heard
goldeneyes—"whistlers"—flying over unseen ... and then
over again, negotiating the fog.

Twenty minutes later the sun burned through, the magpies were warming high in the trees, a three-quarter moon
in the western sky, and the diversions were winter-simple
and thoughtfully spaced. Flickers were down anting on the
sun-softened, south-facing banks of the stream. A snipe
flushed. Two gadwalls jumped from a tiny side-channel
pool that was covered with a layer of new onionskin ice
with a spidery old tumbleweed resting on it; we could see
where they had broken through it in body-wide paths as
they fed along one edge.

And then the first hawk, a dark one, a black one, bolted
out of a bristly cottonwood and was gone, long gone in a
hurry, wanted nothing to do with it, won't be seen again
today by our eyes. Something about it looked like a dark-
phase roughleg. Then we spotted a big female redtail
tucked in a tree sixty yards to the east. She was already
stretching and leaning to peer at us. And another good-
sized bird farther off on a power pole, but doing the same,
keying in on us, alurk, with that perpetual mix of fierce

contempt and well-grounded worry. A few minutes later we found a flurry of small birds in a string of Russian olive trees. Tens of robins and blackbirds, but then a handful of evening grosbeaks, for which the sun heightened a moment on the turmeric-mustard yellows with Mt. Audubon in the skyline background.

And then we saw another hawk, another black one, that had been hidden by thick willows till just then. This one too—the black ones are famously wary—dove from its limb and hurried off but then banked and eased and flew a soft arc around and behind us and finally settled into another would-be low-profile tree back near where we had entered the field. This bird, trim and fast, its tail a blotchy dirty-white, looked like the legendary favorite of black hawks, the Harlan's, and the standard redtails watched it as it went.

When Harlan's hawk was officially reclassified as a subspecies of the redtail thirty years ago, some experienced hawk people questioned the merger. Most all of the black buteos I end up calling Harlan's have a look all their own. Always a lean, leery temperament, as becomes birds reared in the Yukon far from any human company (as opposed to one raised in a ranch shelterbelt or in a tree within earshot of Interstate 25), and a dashing manner. Audubon, who gave the bird its scientific name, knew it as the Black Warrior and considered it "much superior to redtails in flight and daring." Each winter they are back in this part of Colorado with, in my opinion, surprising regularity, having drifted south, from the Mackenzie valley perhaps, along the convenient eastern edge of the Rockies. They show up often in the exact same locales; there is a trio of gnarly old willows four miles from town that holds a Harlan's every year for a month or two. And always with that angular independence and that smoldering, implosive blackness all the handsome dark morphs possess, which seems to add a mystique, the kind of other-option potency held by a white buffalo among the majority herds. ...

We continued down the creek and walked up a knoll that gave us a view of the ponds where a good many ducks were floating in the sun—ringnecks and redheads and enough hooded mergansers to cause a multicar pileup. A dozen gulls rummaged in the muddy-rhinestone ice edges.

We circled near the closest pond, and found another redtail in a tree, dark but not black, just the deep golden-eagle brown of the dark morph western redtail—look again and she's gone—and an odd little two-inch thing in the middle of the trail, a flimsy, colorless device that might have been, we concluded, the backbone from a canned sardine.

But we thought of the black Harlan's all this time, the seasonal specialty, and we often paused to find it in the glasses, way off, still in the same tree. By a certain attention in its distant posture we were sure it hadn't forgotten us either.

When we eventually turned back the way we had come, we wanted it to be there, and it was. We moved toward it at a slow stroll, angling, never going directly at it, even from so far away, and tried to keep incipient eye contact to a minimum. We got quick clear looks at the bird as we moved obliquely closer, could finally make out the patch of white mottling on the breast and see the head begin to pump when it felt our eyes upon it. Then it flushed, couldn't take it—but flew just a few trees west this time.

We walked off at a nonthreatening angle to let the bird relax for a while before we took another good look, and then a final peek from near the car. That all-absorbent carbon/truffle black.

We had been eyeing one another, playing a very elemental game of peekaboo chess on a winter field, for almost an hour, and, not to push the distinguished visitor, not to jangle its fiery Yukon decorum, we quit looking and went home to tend the soup kettle for the rest of the day.

From Summer Notebooks:
Sun Dance Notes

1. Arapaho

The grounds lie in a large open field just east of Ethete, Wyoming. The Wind River range rises to the west. The camp surrounding the sun lodge is a big one with many white tepees among the smaller tents and occasional trailers. Each family camp has erected three-sided sun- and windbreaks of willow boughs lashed onto stalls of poles and boards.

The Northern Arapaho sun dance is esteemed as one of the purest of sun dances. There are guests from all over the West, including a sizable contingent from Oklahoma: Kiowas and of course Southern Arapahos visiting kin in Wyoming. This being Sunday, the final day of the gathering, there are other visitors stopping by. A local priest in black robes and a panama hat stands chatting with friends. A handsome Arapaho girl carrying a large cudgel checks my daypack for camera or recorder.

The chorus of eagle-bone whistles and drum is steady from inside the sun lodge. The aroma of sage pervades the

125

July day. Stacks of fresh-cut reeds for the dancers' resting
beds wait near the entryway. Elders in lawn chairs watch
every move within with alert but not laborious attention.
One old man cries out occasionally, exhorting the dancers.

The Southern Arapaho women stand out in their attire
and carriage. The older ones are dressed up in an unmistakable, pre–World War II Southern way that both defies
and diminishes the afternoon heat. They wear fancy floral
dresses and seamed stockings and permed coiffures with
hairnets over them and carry bright parasols. Their sweet
accents and laughter drift through the camp.

After several hours the near-constant tooting of the
bone whistles becomes a feature of the very day, irrepressi-
ble, like August crickets. As afternoon breaks and the final
evening of dancing begins, the intensity of dancers, singers,
even onlookers heightens subtly.

Gulls sail continually over the lodge, crying, tacking,
casting an eye. ...

What men and women did on the continent today.

July 1987

2. Cheyenne

A high, level meadow enclosed by ponderosa pines, twelve miles south of Lame Deer. The slowly growing camp of tents encircles the glade, hugs the edge of the cooling pines. Mountain bluebirds and crossbills call.

Friday morning: The camp crier on his bay horse rides through camp, publicly summoning members of various men's societies. A dozen of them eventually gather in the middle of the glade and confer, then slowly begin to lay out the sun lodge site, marking it off and soon setting the forked cottonwood uprights with posthole diggers and crowbars.

There is something engaging in the lopped, leafy cotton-wood limbs laid out at the ready on the ground nearby—a compelling image, the idea of a simple common thing cut and handled with ritual care and concern. The stack of them lie there, half wild, half sanctified, leaves still twin-kling in the piney breeze.

Camp sounds gradually intensify: wood being chopped, children at play. Latter afternoon, the crier on his bay horse drags the central sun pole into the skeleton of the lodge; the walls of cottonwood boughs are up. It is complete. Es-sentially, a handful of men from the societies do it all, sus-tain the details of it all through the generations. ...

Friday evening: Suddenly the devotees emerge from the Lone Tepee. Wrapped in blankets or buffalo robes, they proceed slowly, stopping and starting in traditional ritual hesitance. Abraham Spotted Elk directs, quietly and surely. The camp bustle subsides a bit. Then for thirty minutes they circle the lodge in the prescribed formal manner of entry, moving slowly, with their advisers/"grandfathers" at their sides, as the sky takes on a pinkish sundown cast.

The pace is snail slow, with endless consulting between Abraham and his assistants: low talk and pointing, looking around. It has taken all day to raise the sun lodge and get the dancers properly inside, and now the process of trans-formation is well under way. A pleasant glade in the pine woods is steadily transformed into a holy place with the lodge as its sanctified center. The alteration is accomplished through steady, infinitely patient codified action of endless detail, work whose materials are earth, cherry sticks, cotton-wood limbs, the bone of skull. The most daily of things, garnered and shifted to the sacred ...

The camp life and its social sounds comprise a major component of the experience, provide the context that gives the event its public relevance and resonance. The laughter, the squall of children, the cooking smoke from many fires, the racks of sliced meat drying at each campsite, the constant coming and going of low-slung cars and pickups. There are license plates from Oklahoma, Arizona, Wyoming. It is all utterly casual around the camp. Cars honk and teenagers crack wise. Small children are left to their own devices; there is no effort made to impress them with the religious significance of the gathering, though they are occasionally hushed at important moments in the lodge proceedings. Amid this, when there is something to announce, the crier makes his rounds on his bay horse with a far-carrying baritone "Heeey-eey! Heeey-eey!" and proclaims the news in Cheyenne.

Throughout Saturday the transformation builds. The dancers are fully painted and dancing; the eagle whistles pulse all day; the mudhole around the water pump deepens. And by evening, when the inner lodge is illuminated by firelight, the sense of circumscribed sanctum is full: the marked-off, carefully created sanctum. The interior of the lodge—the cottonwood beams, the dancers' willow-bough rest-beds, the shadows moving on the walls—is altered after just a day and a half. The sage on the floor is trampled. It has the feel of a long-occupied, comfortable, receptive place.

The sun dance songs have a hymn-like harmony. Many of them begin very softly, build caressingly, to finally kick in, the eagle whistles joining. I fall asleep to them rising and falling, seventy-five yards away ...

Sunday daybreak: The dancers gather at the eastern door-way of the lodge to dance as the sun rises. Abraham prays silently beside them. The tribal and the American flags flap from a tepee pole. The first sun strikes the inner altar, its buffalo skull, rows of chokecherry sticks, rows of leafy branches stuck in the ground.

Late afternoon: Five dancers go through the piercing: wooden skewers thrust through the skin of the chest and attached with a hide rope to the sun pole or to a heavy buffalo skull. There is gooseflesh through the crowd of onlookers as the struggle to break free begins. After, a man sobs as he em-braces one of the piercers in the lowering sunlight.

What people did on the earth today.

August 1988

For a week following, I held the pace of that patient, generation-after-generation procedure, the measure of distilled Knowing Motion.

And heard remnants of the gentler sun dance songs in my head.

And weeks after, I heard the crier's mellow public exhortatory voice, the calling to attention—"heeey-eey." Resorted to it on occasion during solitary walks on the prairie, used it when saluting a surprise coulee, a change in the wind, a sudden flock of larks.

3. Blackfoot

The camp is set in a mile-wide swale between highway 2 and the railroad tracks, four miles east of Browning. A long crescent drainage-ditch mound lends privacy on the south, the highway side where big trucks roll. The swale is bright green after a wet spring, flecked with flowers. The outermost peaks of Glacier Park are just visible to the northwest.

The camp of dome tents, pickup campers, and vans encircles the Lone Tepee and the open site where the sun lodge will be raised. Three skeletal sun lodge frames from former years stand to the west of camp in various stages of weathering; a few faded offering cloths still toss in the breeze. Pickup trucks come and go with loads of firewood and port-a-johns. One unloads a four-hundred-gallon U.S. Marine Corps water caisson.

A long westbound freight train passes on the northern edge of the grounds, a short half mile from the camp. Meadowlarks and upland plovers sing in the evening sun. The pledger and leaders of the sun dance enter the Lone Tepee for the final night of preparatory singing. Another freight train rolls through. The engineer leans on his elbows at the window of the Burlington Northern engine, checking out the activity—seems to slow a bit. Darkness finally falls at 10 o'clock.

The next morning is cloudy and drizzly, a strong northern odor of alder on the air. A pair of ferruginous hawks is nesting, remarkably, in the upper forks of last year's sun lodge, not far from the new site. One of them frequently sails above the grounds, crying. The people are quietly honored, refer to them as "the eagles." Cars and vans arrive continually: New Mexico, Saskatchewan, Wyoming, Alberta plates. Tepees go up; people are busy preparing sage crown-wreaths and wristlets with red felt wrappings for the dancers.

At midday the sun lodge is marked off with seven-foot aspens stuck in the earth. The outer frame poles have been cut and lie in a rough circle at the perimeter. By midafternoon participants and their families begin to dress. Others test their eagle whistles, blending with the hawk's cries.

Then a large truck pulls in with the sacred center (sun) pole and rafters. They drive in quickly and unload. The sun pole is set with its upper end at rest on a tripod. Four pickups unload piles of aspen boughs: again, that uncanny flash of the wild everyday thing in all its latency, on the verge of transmogrification.

By early evening, all is set, at the ready in a deep stillness. An hour later men are called from the camp and the pole is raised as Buster Yellow Kidney prays beside. There is the intermittent crackle of pre–July Fourth fireworks from dwellings off beyond the highway. Later in the evening, the dancers enter the completed lodge.

The following day the dancing is in full session, the whistles' throbbing soon a part of the morning. The songs seem to be "intertribal": Some are Blackfoot, they say; many are Canadian Cree.

I drive into Browning once or twice a day for food. Some people in town speak in scattered snatches of the sun dance, some challenging its integrity and pastiche style, particularly the number of women and Caucasian dancers (there is a contingent from Chicago, fans of Buster Yellow Kidney). ...

During the day I develop a simple pattern as observer. I stand near the sun lodge entrance for a while, watching the dancers at close hand. Women on one side of the lodge, men on the other. Then I wander off to put some distance on it, take my lawn chair off into the swale to sit alone, or climb the rise just north of the camp and sit there among the swaying flowers and wild roses for an hour. The camp is very lovely from that knoll, spread in afternoon sun, and the sun lodge especially has a great tender beauty from afar, its sloping walls of twelve-foot aspens shimmering in that semisecular, consecrated glow.

Midafternoon the piercing begins. Three men, and then three women, their friends at their sides with tears in their eyes. Silent older men are there to advise, catch the piercers as they break free from the ropes.

After that the peace of early evening is calming. There is a buoyant meadow lull. A soft wind buffets the grasses. Pipits and vesper sparrows sing during the quiet of the sup-per hour. Against the soft sky to the west, the hawks stand out in silhouette on the old sun lodge, the adults hunchbacked and blinking in the rafters, a single woolly young one gaping foul-breathed in the nest.

I stroll up to my favorite knoll and sit on the ground. Smoke from cook fires rises above camp. In a few minutes a seven-year-old girl walks up the slope and presents me shyly with a pork chop and two slices of white bread on a paper plate, a gift from her parents to a visitor, a lingering guest.

At intervals dancers leave the sanctum to walk slowly, their heads covered with blankets, to the pit toilets just east of camp, each accompanied by a helper. They line up and wait their turn silently on the rise.

I finish my pork chop and decide to take a walk, across the meadow to the railroad tracks. There I sit beside a willow clump and smoke, and weep for a minute, and smoke again, amid the pretty yarrow and red-eyed susans and horse droppings.

I hear the eagle whistles begin again from the distant lodge. If prayer rises, this must be something like the sun hears. Then a big westbound train goes through, loaded piggyback with Hanjin and Mitsui freight cars.

What men and women did on the earth today.

June 1990

Works Consulted

Basho. *The Narrow Road to the Deep North and Other Travel Sketches.* Translated by Nobuyuki Yuasa. Penguin, 1966. The poem quoted on page 24 is from "The Records of a Weather-Exposed Skeleton."

Bent, Arthur C. *Life Histories of North American Birds,* various volumes. Dover Publications.

Burroughs, John. *Fresh Fields.* The Riverside Press, 1896.

Duncan, Robert. *Roots and Branches.* Scribners, 1964. The poem quoted on page 114 is "Returning to the Rhetoric of an Early Mode."

Forbush, Edward Howe, and John Bichard May. *A Natural History of American Birds.* Bramhall House, 1974.

Hodge, Frederick W., ed. *Handbook of American Indians North of Mexico.* Bureau of American Ethnology, 1906.

Mathews, F. Schuyler. *Fieldbook of Wild Birds and Their Music.* Putnam's, 1905.

Mertz, Henriette. *Pale Ink.* N.p., 1953.

Sauer, Carl O. *Selected Essays, 1963–1975.* Turtle Island Foundation, 1981.

Singh, Raghubir. *Ganga: Sacred River of India*. Perennial Press, 1974.

Tomelleri, Joseph, and Mark Eberle. *Fishes of the Central United States*. University Press of Kansas, 1990.

Twain, Mark. *The Writings of Mark Twain*. Harper, 1922–1925.

Williams, William Carlos. *Selected Poems*. New Directions, 1963. The poem quoted on page 83 is "Flowers by the Sea."